Collecting
Quilts
Investments in America's Heritage

Cathy Gaines Florence

Shown is the display booth set up at the Michigan Depression Glass Society show held in October, 1983, at the Dearborn Civic Center. This lovely display was designed by Ms. Pat Mitchell.

The red and white **Crown and Thorns** quilt (also known as Wedding Ring, Single Wedding Ring, Grandmother's Wedding Ring, Wheel, Rolling Stone, Block Circle, Georgetown Circle and Memory Wreath) is owned by Mrs. Virginia Willmont; the **Butterfly,** beside the Shirley Temple doll, belongs to Ms. Carolyn Kugler.

I wish to thank the Society President, Mr. Ken Godwin, and the Show Chairpersons, Norma Godwin and Marge Truscott for allowing us to photograph the display for use in this book.

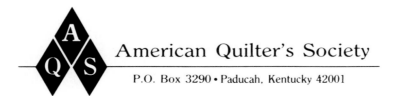
American Quilter's Society

P.O. Box 3290 • Paducah, Kentucky 42001

The current values in this book should be used as a guide. They are not intended to set prices, which vary from one section of the country to another. Auction prices as well as dealer prices vary greatly and are affected by condition as well as demand. Neither the Author nor the Publisher assumes responsibility for any losses that might be incurred as a result of consulting this guide.

Additional copies of this book may be ordered from

AMERICAN QUILTER'S SOCIETY
P. O. Box 3209
Paducah, Kentucky 42001

or

Cathy Gaines Florence
P. O. Box 22186
Lexington, Kentucky 40522

@$19.95 per copy. When ordering by mail, please add $1.00 to cover postage and handling.

Copyright: Cathy Gaines Florence, 1985
ISBN: 0-89145-282-6

DEDICATION

To the creators of all the beauty,
love and warmth shown herein
and to my grandmothers
who taught me to appreciate it

THANKS TO . . .

I could make a book of names of people to thank. They are legion! Strangers have become friends who have gone "above and beyond" to be supportive and lend help, to get quilts to me and for me. We have invaded their homes and disrupted their lives with our camera and our curiosity about their collections. I haven't praises enough for the overwhelming generosity of spirit we've been privileged to experience. By way of thanks, I have tried to list everyone's name by the photograph of his or her quilt. I have particularly tried to stress the names of dealers whom I found to be knowledgeable and helpful to me in the extreme. (Quilts not acknowledged belong to me.)

I especially need to thank photographer Bob Anstett, of Wilmore, Kentucky, who loaned us his studio (and helped give my husband a crash course in photography up to and including exact shutter speeds, light readings and distances at which they all work best) when it was discovered that it would be totally impossible to get all the quilts we encountered photographed at one time in a formal studio setting. We were going to "miss" too many quilts that way. We needed on-site shots nine out of ten times.

I wish to thank dealer Sharon Boren of New Albany, Ohio, who offered her lovely quilts to me for photographing. Time ran out before I got to them, unfortunately, but I cherish her offer of help.

I am grateful to Malcolm Barry of Ohio and Sally Dryman who helped me secure special types of quilts for the book.

I need to thank my father, a "genius," as one dealer described him after seeing the frame he built to hold the quilts for photographing. The frame had to be of giant proportions, able to travel, easy to set up and it had to hold quilts against the wind. Charles Gaines definitely came to our rescue in that department!

I want to thank my mother, Sibyl Gaines, and my aunt, Renae Juett, who traveled with me various times to view quilts. They directed me over unfamiliar routes and helped carry garbage-bagged loads of quilts.

I thank my children who tried hard to be understanding of parents gone when they needed them, of hasty sandwiches instead of regular meals, of a living room piled with quilts and dark as a tomb for weeks on end. (When winter came, we could no longer photograph outside; so we moved the furniture out of our family living area and made it an impromptu studio, spending DAYS pinning, photographing, and unpinning quilts.) We all suffered through this seemingly endless task.

My husband has served as my "other half" countless times - at markets finding quilts, at home getting meals, at an interview asking the right questions, behind the camera snapping photographs. He's always encouraged me; he's pushed when I lagged; and he's slowed me when I approached exhaustion. Without him, there would have been no book.

I also acknowledge my dependence on my Heavenly Father who was daily, unfailingly sufficient to His daughter's innermost needs.

COUNCIL

A friend once asked a realtor the three most important things to consider when buying property. The realtor answered without hesitation, "Location, location, location." In that same spirit, the three most important things to consider when buying a quilt are, "Condition, condition, condition." Age, rarity of design, amount of quilting thread used, fineness of stitching, etc., mean practically nothing if the quilt isn't in good condition. Holes, tears, missing fabrics, fading and repairs (no matter how skillful) all indicate quilts of less-than-average condition and should be priced and purchased accordingly.

WHY THIS BOOK . . .

We were in the publisher's office when suddenly he looked across the desk at me and said, "I want you to write a book on quilts!"

I must've looked negative, because he held up his hand and continued, "Now, before you say, 'No!', let me finish. I've been reading every quilt book I could lay my hands on for the last six months, and there isn't anything out there like I want. First, I want a book in color, not one of those cheap little books with black and white, postage-stamp size pictures of quilts. I want a book where you can see the quilt! Next, I want it to be a price guide, with prices right there by the quilt, not over in the back where you have to keep flipping and hunting to find them; and I'd rather have actual prices, not "X, Y, Z" codes. I want a book that an antiques dealer or collector can buy, and read and gain enough knowledge to go out in the market and feel reasonably certain he knows enough to intelligently buy a quilt!" Then, he grinned. "I haven't quite decided how all that can be done, but that's what I want; and I believe you're the one who can put it together for me." He sat there beaming and looking expectantly toward me.

I asked, "Do you have any idea how much MORE travel that would involve?"

"Well, maybe a little more than you all do already; but the beauty of this is that you and Gene go to these markets all over the country anyway. So, while he's looking for new items and prices in Depression Glass, you can be checking out the quilts." He shifted in his seat and leaned forward. "You can do that for me anyway, whether you decide to write the book or not. See what kinds of quilts are really out there for sale. I know these museum pieces they photograph in most of these books aren't your everyday market quilts. Check with some dealers; get a feel for the market. Find out what people would like to see in a quilt book and let me know the results!"

All I agreed to do was to "check out the market" . . . !

One year, some 25,000 miles and 2,200 work-hours later, having visited over 40 markets, shows, exhibits or museums in connection with the quilt research; having driven from Michigan to Texas, from Kansas to Pennsylvania, and from Florida to all the states between photographing quilts; having read all of my publisher's books on quilts and more; and having spent a year's salary buying quilts so that we'd know at exactly what prices dealers are willing to part with their quilts, this is the result.

I gave it my best effort and I hope it will be of value to you.

FOREWORD . . .

Coming from a long line of quilters (my grandmothers, great-grandmothers, aunts and a great-aunt, Lill(y) Gill, who, in ten days, could "put in" and "take out" a quilt filled with tiny, even stitches), I thought that I knew something about quilts!. It didn't take long for me to discover my knowledge was woefully inadequate; so, I began to read every book and article I could find regarding quilts.

I soon realized that I was reading the same material and seeing the same quilts pictured over and over. I decided I would show quilts that hadn't been photographed before and I'd leave the telling of the history of quilts to those authors who have already told it so well and in such volume. (You can find this information at your local library. It's interesting reading, but rehashing it here would take space from the photos; and time and again I was told by quilters and collectors, "Just show us quilts!")

Further, as I viewed book after book, I saw only excellent grade quilts. In a book of the type my publisher had outlined, all grades of quilts should be shown, so that potential dealers and collectors could gain a REAL knowledge of what is available in today's market.

I tried to show quilts from as many areas of the country (though I admit to a preponderance of those from Kentucky and the surrounding states) and in as many different patterns as was possible.

Because I have always been able to learn material better by placing it in chronological order, I attempted to show the quilts that way rather than leaping from date to date as do many other books. I also tried to show typical patterns, styles of quilting, fabrics and colors in their time frame.

I took the liberty of listing various pattern names of **like designs** together, knowing that they were not all pieced in the same fashion. (One pattern may have a square, the other may make that square **design** from two triangles sewn together; yet the **design** is the same—a square!)

The value guide is just that, a guide. These prices are by no means written in concrete, nor are they all mine. Sometimes dealers and owners suggested prices which, for the most part, I accepted. It gives the pricing a broader base of reference and expertise than one person could give and I felt it would be of more value to you. Something is really "worth" whatever someone else is willing to pay for it and not necessarily the value at which it is "booked." **The values are frames of reference to guide your own judgment.** Generally speaking, New York, Texas and California quilt markets tend to command higher prices than do those in mid-America.

TABLE OF CONTENTS

YEARS

TYPES

1775 - 1799

Photo # 1

Design: Star of Le Moyne
Type: Patchwork, self-edged border (back over front)
Size: 73¼″ x 85¼″
Maker: "Grandmother Stevens' mother"
Date: c. 1775
Condition: Poor; surface browns crumbling and missing; linen backing good
Quilting: Diagonal lines and ¾″ squares; 8 stitches per inch
Value: $250.00 - $500.00; mostly historical

Comments: This was the oldest quilt I was able to find in my year's search to discover just what quilts are available RIGHT NOW to the person beginning to collect. Indeed, that's the whole premise of this book, to see what is still available to the modern-day collector. Have all the really good quilts been taken? Are they all locked away in museums and collections of years standing? Or, are there quilts of genuine investment potential still to be had? Where do you find them? What are they selling for right now?

This quilt from Atwater, Ohio, has a letter attached to it which is dated "Thurs., Nov. 2, 1922" and states that the quilt was owned originally by "grandmother Stevens" who was "grandmother Hatfield's grandmother. Grandmother Hatfield was born in 1803 and lived to be over 90 years of age." It further states that the quilt was probably made in England. Allowing 20 years per generation from 1922, the quilt would have a 1780's date. Allowing the three generations back from the 1803 date would put it closer to 1740.

Although my knowledge of this quilt maker is limited, I know she had long, silky "strawberry blonde" hair. I found a tiny end protruding and pulled. The center padding yielded a strand of her hair. It was so embedded, it had to have been caught there as the quilt was first sewn together.

I bought this at a flea market from a dealer who said it had been in a camel-back trunk he had bought at a spinster lady's estate sale. Most collectors (just as that day at the market) wouldn't touch this with a barge pole because of the obvious deterioration of the brown fabric with the chartreuse green splotches as design. I found the materials a textbook education in 18th century fabrics; plus, I thought it a fitting start for the book. The quilt may have come from England, having English block designed fabrics. Most of our early fabrics in the so-called "American made" quilts did likewise.

The "Le Moyne" star design was a favorite pattern in America. It was based on the crest of two French-Canadian brother explorers. In 1699, one brother, Pierre, the Sieur d'Iberville helped found colonies near what are now Biloxi, Mississippi, and Mobile, Alabama. Pierre died of a fever in 1706 at age 45. The other, Jean Baptiste, Sieur de Bienville, settled some French colonists by Lake Pontchartrain in 1718 and called the settlement New Orleans. When Napoleon abruptly decided to sell the French holdings in America, trade flooded down the Mississippi and ladies were quick to notice the Le Moyne crest as a design worthy of their quilts. Two hundred years later, their "flag still flies" in quilts throughout the land!

Some fabric designs in the stars: a red/pink fleur de lis symbol with a blue base on a medium brown background; blue leaves with tiny dotted edges beside it; many brown-toned backgrounds with jagged Granddaddy Long Legs spider-type vines connecting buff-colored leaves and flowers. There's a resist dyed indigo blue with a tiny white branch made of dots. The madder root-dyed pink material has a resist "star" but a printed brown dot square.

Photo # 2

Design: Nine Patch
Type: Patchwork
Size: 100″ x 101″
Maker: Mrs. Morrison (Venton County, Ohio)
Date: c. 1795
Condition: Excellent
Quilting: Winding leaf and shell-patterned; even but large stitching
Value: $2,000.00 - $2,500.00

Comments: The previous owner "remembered" this as having been made in "1780 or 1790". It has a three piece backing of a basket-weave material that could be fustian. It is unlined, having been made as a cover or spread. The brown material with white flowers is very like some fabrics seen in a quilt made by Martha Washington presently housed in the museum at Mt. Vernon.

Photo # 1

Photo # 2

7

Photo # 3

Design: **Lone Star** (earlier names: Rising Sun and Star of Bethlehem)
Type: Patchwork and applique "Masterpiece" quilt, self-edged border
Size: 103½" x 108½"
Maker: Unknown, found in Lexington, Kentucky (garage sale)
Date: c. 1825
Condition: Brown colors deteriorated or gone
Value: $1,500.00 - $2,200.00

Comments: They say the Australian aborigines have a reverential respect for anything old. That was the effect this quilt had on us at the studio when we stretched it across the frame and stood it up before the camera. You had to "look up to it" not only in fact, but in feeling. The backing of the quilt, possibly home spun, is in very good shape. It's giant size indicates it was made to cover the wider and taller beds in use up to about the 1850's. (Three-quarter beds were first introduced after the War of 1812, but not widely used until much later.) Covers, then, were required to be of sufficient proportions to hide the trundle beds beneath and the mountains of feather ticking above. Only an expert seamstress would tackle this pattern on this giant scale. Lone Star diamonds tend to stretch and creep out of shape in incompetent hands.

The border fabric is of a type that was manufactured about 1825, having urns and flowers in soft hues of red and brown on a tea-colored background and edged by intricate, scrolled (arabesque) designs.

This quilt needs some reweaving work done near the urns. I understand this is expensive; but I believe the quilt worthy of the expense. Due to the iron oxide used in making the brown dye, much of the brown material used in the star has deteriorated. These areas could simply be netted. (Deterioration/disintegration of brown dyed materials is common to older fabrics because of the dye salts eating away at the fabric.)

Photo # 3 Courtesy Flag Fork Antiques, Frankfort, Ky.

Photo # 4

Design: Blazing Star and Diamonds
Type: Patchwork; block print on linen
Size: 81″ x 64″
Maker: Unknown
Date: c. 1820
Condition: Excellent
Value: $900.00 - $1,000.00

Comments: This was utilitarian, but decorative. The use of flowered prints and a zigzag border are a testament to the quilter's desire for beauty. A judicious placement of the contrasting fabrics with a view to the overall harmony of design credit this quilter's artistic "eye." Use of these same contrasting fabrics speak also of the frugality of the maker's nature.

Photo # 5

Design: Double Nine Patch
Type: Patchwork, Crib
Size: 34″ x 48″
Maker: Attributed to the Isaac Shelby family
Date: 1834
Condition: Good
Value: $700.00 - $900.00

Comments: Notice the pink, plaid/check fabric; curled, stylized leaves; the use of lavendar, brown, rose and purple (now faded to brown tones); the use of stripes, especially the "ribbon" border where the lavendar and rose colors shade into each other without intervening lines. All these "signs" are typical of the machine rolled prints of the second quarter of the 19th century.
   Many crib quilts are worth as much, or more, than full size quilts.

Photo # 4 Courtesy Shelly Zegart's Quilts, Louisville, Ky.

Photo # 5 Courtesy Shelly Zegart's Quilts, Louisville, Ky.

11

Photo # 6

Design: Urn With Flowers
Type: Applique with embroidered flower stems
Size: 77" x 98"
Maker: Margaret Conger, Shelbyville, Indiana
Date: 1838
Quilting: Diagonal lines, ¼" apart; done by Jeannette Conger and her mother, Mary Jane Conger in 1858 at Casey, Indiana
Value: $2,000.00 - $2,500.00

Comments: Urns with flowers were popular "commercial" designs (fabric wall paper) from the early 1800's; it was only natural that they should be adapted by the quilter. Notice the reds and true greens on pure white, the still vibrant yellow and pink dotted with red. It is interesting to notice that the center urn's yellow flower appears to have at one time been half green (hand dyed blue over yellow). This was evidently an attempt toward an obvious flaw, a superstitious, moral obligation to make a deliberate mistake since only God could make "perfect" things. It was all right to strive toward perfection, just not to achieve it. That was too "high and mighty" an attitude and would doubtless lead to destruction of one's soul.

Photo # 7

Design: Possibly **Cherries**
Type: Applique
Maker: Sally Clark, Owen Co., Kentucky
Date: c. 1840
Condition: Some fading of leaves; some worn red appliques; some "boxing"
Value: $125.00 - $225.00

Comments: Boxing is a condition in which a chemical reaction takes place between the wood in the storage container and the fabric which results in the fabric turning brown and eventually deteriorating. Ideally, quilts should be rolled and stored in cloth sleeves so they can "breathe"; plastic bags, temperature extremes and undue moisture, as in a basement, should be avoided. Whatever the design, it has been seen on a quilt dated 1855 which points to the fact that it was a pattern "in vogue" at the time and not one "made up" by Sally Clark. It has been suggested that it might be tomatoes since they were considered poisonous and good only for the flower gardens of the day. I think the way the fruit is "cupped" by the leaves precludes that, even allowing for stylization of said tomato leaves.

The "green" in the fabric of the leaves has returned mostly to blue color. This is the type of quilt that is dearer to the family than to a collector. However, once on the market, it is also the type that can be successfully reworked for further service. With soaking (not bleach!), the "boxing" stains can be lightened or removed, appliques can be patched over (not removed!) and borders can be added to enhance or enlarge the quilt to required spread size. I realize "adding to" or "touching" an antique quilt in ANY manner will be viewed as heresy by some. Yet, I have seen so many of these types of quilts sitting in markets, neglected or destined to become pillows, skirts, teddy bears, pigs and ducks, that I'm compelled to say there is life here YET as a QUILT.

Photo # 8

Design: North Caroliona Lily Variation
Type: Applique
Size: 70" x 87"
Maker: Unknown
Date: c. 1850
Condition: Applique worn through; border frayed; some stains
Quilting: Very fine; double feather quilting in border; center medallions
Value: $75.00 - $125.00

Comments: Materials are green with yellow dots and red with white dots; numerous cotton seeds are found in the lining. The undulating flower border is typical of this time. The quilt could be "restored" by recovering the appliques since the backings and quilting are still in good shape. Use of the white background indicates it was used as the "best" quilt.

Photo # 6 Courtesy Dr. John Caton, Frankfort, Ky

Photo # 7 Courtesy Betty Gayle Kenney, Owenton, Ky.

Photo # 8 Courtesy Joy Newman, Ashland, Ohio

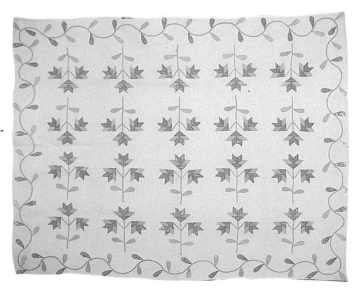

Photo # 9, 10, 11

Design: **Four Stars** (similar to Jackson Star)
Type: Trapunto (stuffed) patchwork
Size: 76" x 87"
Maker: Unknown
Date: c. 1845
Condition: Rebound, design appliqued over original, stuffed work hanging in several places from surface fabric tears
Quilting: Above average; 9 to 10 stitches per inch
Value: $400.00 - $600.00 (in mint condition $6,000.00 - $8,000.00)

Comments: Stuffed work quilts are known to have been made for nearly 600 years. However, most of the ones still in existence in America date from the late 1700's. They were formed by sewing two fabrics together in a design, then carefully parting the loosely woven stitches of the backing fabric and poking in cotton wading with a crochet hook or large needle.

Some dealers make a distinction between "stuffed" work and the Italian corded quilting (drawing cord through the design) known as trapunto. Since most of these type quilts have both stuffing and cording (as does this one), "trapunto" has come to be the term used by most dealers for either type work.

The original binding that remains on this quilt appears to have been dyed green by mixing yellow and blue. The binding is decidedly blue now. (Any time a quilt is rebound, the original binding should be undistrubed if at all possible to preserve its authenticity--and antique value!)

The shape of the stuffed urn, the profusion of designs [grapes, leaves, strawberries, a sunflower, a pineapple (the age old symbol of hospitality)], the colors, red and green on white, even the extreme "C" ended scrolls in the edge of the design help "date" this quilt. I searched in vain for a date or a signature in the actual quilting itself.

I found this tired, but still beautiful gem at Stewart's Flea Market in Louisville, Kentucky. It had been willed to a university by one of its professors and subsequently sold to provide funds for a new building. The professor was probably responsible for the rebinding and the 1930's cloth re-applique of the stars. Underneath that now-faded-to-pink star is the original red material which has tiny, short repeat blue flowers outlined in white. Most of the blue color is gone.

Photo #9

Photo #10

Photo #11

15

Photo # 12

Design: **Multiple designs**
Type: Applique Baltimore Album
Maker: Eleanor A. Gorshuch
Date: c. 1850
Condition: Good to Excellent; never used
Quilting: Very fine; tiny diamonds; trapunto cherries
Value: Appraised: $18,500.00

Comments: This was made by the above young lady from Baltimore County while in attendance at Gorshuch College. In that time frame, her courses were probably advanced needlework techniques, the art of water coloring, and the pianoforte. She definitely deserved an "A" in sewing class! The work is "quilled" (signed) once by her mother, Elizabeth, and once by Eleanor. (One signature is on the card in the basket; the other is beneath the Eagle.) Other quill work includes "feathering" around the grapes.

As Eleanor never married, she passed this down to a favorite nephew and, subsequently, it has gone to the "Eleanors" in the family. When she first gave it, it was merely a skillfully worked quilt. Today, it's a family heirloom and a legacy.

Baltimore Album quilts are highly prized by collectors. One lecturer I heard estimated there are only 40 or 50 known to exist. It is believed either a society of ladies in Baltimore made these various motifs and sold them to provide funds for some project or that one lady did these to supplement her income; hence so few in existence.

A Baltimore Album quilt recently sold for $26,000.00.

Photo # 12 Courtesy Private Collector. Photo supplied by writer Daphne Ginnings, Akron *Beacon Journal*

Photo # 13

Design: **Unknown, probably original;** (Royal Star and Palm Flower?)
Type: Patchwork and applique
Size: 74″ x 90″
Maker: The Keller sisters, Centralia, Illinois
Date: 1851
Condition: Poor; materials worn and missing; quilting later than top; poster bed cut outs filled in with different material
Value: $100.00 - $200.00

Comments: This pattern no doubt originated with these sisters who made it for their brother, a minister. They've filled it with religious symbolism, much of which is speculative at this point. The blood red cross is a ''bleeding heart'' or ''royal'' pattern star; the flowers could either be variations of ''Hosanna'' or ''Palm leaf'' pattern; or they could simply be tulips, a recognized symbol of love at that time. There are ''lillies'' in the border stemming from the star and there's a triangular motif with red dots at each point which was supposed to represent the Trinity. The circle of white in the center of the star could be anything . . . the circle of life, love, purity; and the Le Moyne stars throughout represent celestial dwellers if nothing else.

Were the quilt in good condition, it would be worth two to three thousand dollars due to uniqueness of design. I bought it in this sad state thinking that by featuring it here, I might somehow help ''preserve'' their design.

It is dated 1851 with spidery thin, tiny cross stitching worked in brown thread. Tiny cross stitching was one of the typical ways of registering dates on a quilt during this time period.

Photo # 14

Design: **Wandering Foot** (later Turkey Tracks)
Type: Patchwork and applique
Size: 80¼″ x 102″
Maker: Hallie Rice of Salyersville, Kentucky
Date: c. 1855
Condition: Average; but flawed by having been cut down for a smaller bed at some point!
Quilting: Diamonds (intersecting lines, ¼″ apart)
Value: $250.00 - $400.00

Comments: There's an obvious flaw in that one ''track'' turns outward in the corner swag. There's a quilter's error regarding the size of the swags. You would hardly have noticed this as the quilt lay on a bed; but hanging, it is noticeable. To me, it adds to the charm of the quilt. To some meticulous collectors, however, this would put them off buying it.

The main damage was done by some ancestor who wanted to use it and didn't have a bed with the grand dimensions the quilt required. She carefully cut two sections of the design off and then at some later time, resewed them. The cut-off portion naturally has a newer look. As it's a family-owned quilt, this merely adds interest to the family lore. Had this NOT been done, the quilt today would be worth $1,250.00 - $1,800.00.

There's quilting of leaves, pineapples and medallions. The swags were sewn with colored ''green'' thread that is now turning blue. This may be an indication of hand dyed (blue and yellow) thread since manufacturers had had true green color since about 1810 and were using it prolifically from 1837. This notion is enhanced by the presence of a homespun backing. There are cotton seeds showing in the batting; the stitches are an average of eight per inch.

Photo # 13

Photo # 14 Courtesy Mr. and Mrs. Maurice Rice, Lexington, Ky.

19

Photo # 15, 16

      Design: **Coxcomb Variation**
        Type: Applique
        Size: Large: 84″ x 84″; Small: (crib quilt or pillow sham) 35″ x 45″
     Maker: Attributed to Richter (German) family, Sunman, Indiana
       Date: Large: 1852; Small: 1856
 Condition: Good to Excellent; some small stains
   Quilting: Diamonds
     Value: $4,000.00 - $5,500.00 (pair)

      Comments: Quilts with "Pennsylvania Dutch" or German influences are of particular interest to collectors. They are usually filled with bright, cheerful colors and often feature birds, hearts, tulips and various "hex" signs as quilting motifs; and they are generally extremely well-executed.

It is unusual to find like pieces unless pillow shams were made to match the master quilt; and in those instances, there are two pieces. Tradition has it that this smaller one was made for a new baby's bed; the color variation here seems to bear this out.

Red birds were often ascribed to marriage and baby quilts signifying the hope for a happy life (flying above life's worries and problems.)

Photo # 17

      Design: **Coxcomb**
        Type: Applique
        Size: 93½″ x 94″
     Maker: Signed, "L. H. Meyer"
       Date: c. 1858
 Condition: Good
   Quilting: Diamonds; 12-13 stitches per inch
     Value: $800.00 - $1,100.00

      Comments: Cotton seed batting; lovely quilting; bought in Pennsylvania.

Photo # 18

      Design: **Lone Star** (Star of Bethlehem) center;
               Harvest Sun (Prairie Star, Ship's Wheel) corners
               Saw Tooth (Bear's Tooth) border
        Type: Patchwork
        Size: 86″ x 87″
     Maker: Dr. Scott's wife, Burlington, Iowa
       Date: c. 1858
 Condition: Excellent
     Value: $2,200.00 - $2,500.00

      Comments: This design is enhanced by the circular movement the quilter achieved via use of color and the "joining" of the star points, all obviously the work of a skilled craftsman.

Photo # 15 and 16 Courtesy Steven Jenkins and Dave Cowden, Indianapolis, Ind.

Photo # 17 Courtesy Bill and Bunny Nolt, Worthington, Ohio

Photo # 18 Courtesy Spirit of America, St. Louis, Mo.

Photo # 19, 20

Design: **Lone Star of Paradise** (Double Star, Unknown Star, Carpenter's Wheel, Star Within A Star; other similar patterns include: Dutch Rose, Octagonal Star and Broken Star)
Type: Patchwork ''marriage'' quilt
Size: 96" x 104"
Maker: Matilda Boyd, Mason County, Kentucky
Date: c. 1857
Condition: Excellent
Quilting: Diamonds and straight lines so close as to appear stippled; petaled flowers; 10-11 stitches per inch
Value: $2,500.00 - $3,500.00

Comments: This quilt has an unusual feature in that welting appears in the border, that is, an additional strip of fabric has been placed between the border and the body of the quilt. Tiny red and green welted borders have been found mostly on quilts made in Kentucky, Virginia and England, indicating an historical origin for this custom. In this case, the red welting carries out her red/green theme, even in the binding. It has a three piece (plus a scrap) backing of what appears to be homespun material; cotton seed batting; a linen marking tag quilled ''A F'' or ''E H Boyd'' on the back, possibly the son she intended to inherit the quilt; and it is signed on the face of the quilt, ''M B'' under ''H C B''. At the moment, no one in the family can supply HIS name.

Documentation lends value to a quilt. One dealer said it means as much as a third again of the price; another flatly said documentation doubles the value of a quilt. Thus, it is important to take the time to find out the history of a quilt. If you ARE a quilter, you should sign and date your work via a cloth tag attached to the back. (Never pin tags with safety pins; they collect moisture and rust on the fabric in a very short time!) If you are in possession of a family quilt and know the history of its making, write it out on paper, place the paper in a plastic bag and slip stitch the bag to the quilt. Without having done this book, I would NEVER have known the history behind our family quilts. None of it was written. All was stored in the memory of my grandmothers, both of whom are past 80 years of age.

Photo # 19

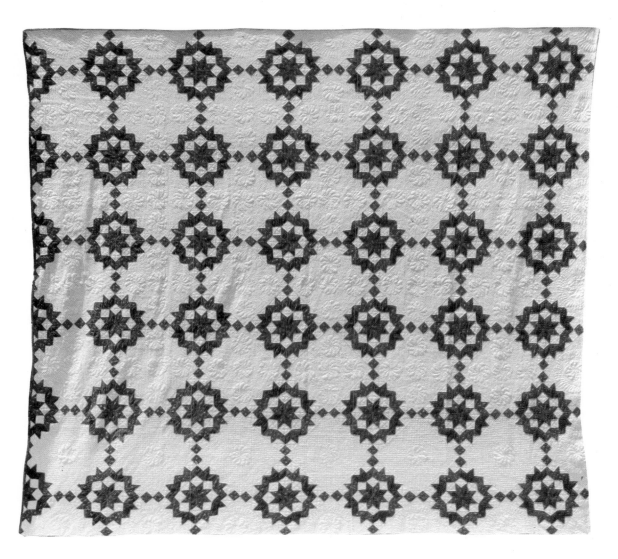

Photo # 20

Photo # 21

Design: Rose Cross
Type: Applique
Size: 88″ x 89″
Maker: Mother of Eliza Masten Beatty, Ohio
Date: c. 1860
Condition: Poor; repaired in center; some leaf fabric missing
Quilting: Excellent; ¼″ diamonds, feathered leaves with stippled centers
Value: $225.00 - $325.00

Comments: The ancestry of this quilt was attached to it. It reaches six generations back from John and Doug Grissinger to the above. The center section of the quilt was reputedly damaged by some family dogs scratching it in preparation to lying down. Had these animals not lain in such splendor, the quilt would be worth $1,000.00 to $1,500.00 today! The outlying portions of the quilt are in good condition; even the fabrics still retain good coloring.

Photo # 22

Design: Oak Leaf and Feather (Rose)
Type: Applique
Size: 74 ″ x 75¼″
Maker: Unknown; but religious; two flowers are ''flawed'' white
Date: c. 1865
Condition: Average; binding worn; green fading to yellow in places
Quilting: Double lines, ¼″ apart at inch intervals, shell quilting between the flowers
Value: $225.00 - $350.00

Comments: The ¼″, SEPARATE binding is machine stitched with tiny stitches (the type early machines stitched.)
  An Englishman, Thomas Saint, FIRST invented a sewing machine in 1790; however, it only produced a single thread chain stitch. In 1830, Bartholomy Thimmonier of France and in 1832, Walter Hunt, an American, produced the first lock stitch machines. However, it is Elias Howe, with a much-improved version patented in 1846, who is universally credited with the invention; and it took a Mr. Singer to really mass-market the invention by offering installment credit to buyers. Sewing machines weren't generally found in American homes until after the Civil War. A sewing machine was truly a ''status symbol!'' Actual ''quilting'' with them proved more of a chore than hand quilting due to bunching of the layers of material under the presser foot and having to baste the layers so thoroughly. Many an expert needlewoman, however, proudly sewed on appliques and bindings with the machine! Often they used contrasting thread color so you'd be certain to see the machine stitching!
  I find it laughable that some collectors turn down beautifully hand-crafted quilts from this era ''because it's been machine bound!'' How silly! To me, it's ''icing on the cake'' — a further verification of the product!

Photo # 23, 24

Design: ''Rose'' (name unknown)
Type: Applique
Size: 81″ x 90½″
Maker: Unknown
Date: c. 1865
Condition: Good; some greens fading to blue
Quilting: Triple diagonal lines
Value: $800.00 - $1,100.00

Comments: We turned this to the sun and took a picture from behind to show you the tiny cotton seeds that are visible in older quilts. This one has few, an indication of a Southern-made quilt so ''they'' say. Northern quilts tend to have more seeds due to the absence of gins and slaves to pick them out by hand. These seed oils often have seeped through the materials causing a condition known as ''foxing,'' or slight brown areas where the seeds are located. This ''foxing'' isn't considered alarming among collectors.
  As you can see, this was the ''era'' of appliqued quilts. There are numerous ones still available and in good condition. You will have several choices; so you may take the time to ''like'' one particularly.

Photo # 21

Photo # 22

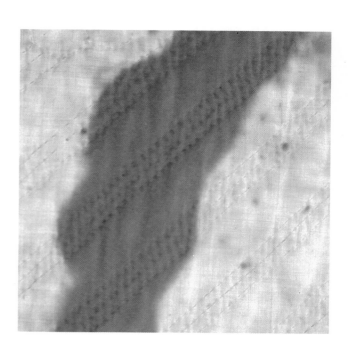

Photo # 23, 24 Courtesy Alice Warobiew, Brookfield, Ohio

25

Photo # 25, 26

Design: Kentucky Rose Variation
Type: Applique and patchwork with embroidery
Size: 85¼" x 85¼"
Maker: Susan (Mrs. George) Churchill, Larue County, Kentucky
Date: c. 1860
Condition: Average to Good; fading of some home-dyed thread used in embroidery
Quilting: Diagonal lines, ¼" apart; 10 stitches per inch
Value: $2,000.00 - $2,500.00

Comments: This quilt has a three-piece backing of what appears home spun material and a cotton seed batting. The flower is made of eight pieces using four fabrics; each pieced and then appliqued. Pineapples and leaves are quilted in the white blocks; with dark brown thread used to quilt the flower.

Legend passed with the quilt says that some of Abraham Lincoln's relatives helped with the quilting. Due to the age and finding it in his home territory, it's very believable though not yet documented as fact. We took a picture of the quilt by Lincoln's boyhood home cabin at Knob Creek, hoping to accentuate what a note of cheer a quilt could bring to its surroundings!

Photo # 27, 28

Design: Tulips (symbol of love)
Type: Applique and patchwork
Size: 89" x 96"
Maker: Unknown; but from Hardin County, Kentucky
Date: c. 1865
Condition: Excellent
Quilting: Diamonds; pineapple motifs in plain squares
Value: $2,500.00 - $3,000.00

Comments: This is one of the most meticulously quilted works I've ever been privileged to view.

Photo # 25, 26

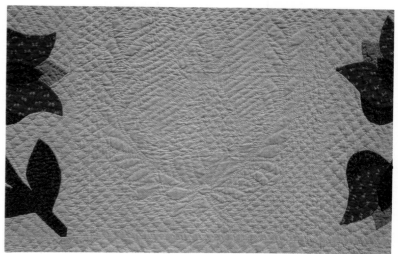

Photo # 27, 28 Courtesy Mrs. Frank Lovell, Versailles, Ky.

1850 - 1874

Photo # 29

Design: Basket of Flowers
Type: Applique
Size: 76" x 76"
Maker: Attributed to Brelage family, Dubois County, Indiana
Date: c. 1860
Condition: Good; some faint spotting
Quilting: Excellent; feather swag borders; flower medallions; ¼" diagonal lines; other fancy fretworks around the flower buds
Value: $800.00 - $1,200.00

Comments: This basket design was popular in this region during this time frame. The designs aren't totally symetrical; this merely acknowledges that human hands made this. There are three leaves in the "border" of leaves of another color. They may have been set in deliberately "flawed".

Photo # 30

Design: Grapes?
Type: Applique
Size: 60" x 70"
Maker: Unknown
Date: c. 1870
Condition: Average; doubtless the leaves have faded from green to yellow
Quilting: Good; medallions in white areas
Value: $350.00 - $500.00

Comments: Unusual design set together without any regard for symmetry. It's one of those quilts that surely was an "original" and is so bizarre as to be of note. Placed here primarily to show the tendency toward using tan colored fabrics from the early 1860's to the 1880's.

Photo # 31

Design: Rose Wreath Variation
Type: Applique and patchwork with embroidery
Size: 82" x 82"
Maker: Pennsylvanian
Date: c. 1865
Condition: Good
Quilting: Double line
Value: $1,200.00 - $1,500.00

Comments: Tulips are pieced; center flower is buttonhole stitch embroidery. The Rose Wreath was a standard applique design of the time; however, the addition of the tulips is defintely a Pennsylvania "Dutch" touch.

Photo # 32

Design: Love Apple (in a bud and bloom arrangement)
Type: Applique
Size: 82" x 82"
Maker: Unknown
Date: c. 1870
Condition: Good
Quilting: ½" squares; large, feathered medallions
Value: $800.00 - $1,200.00

Comments: The bowls of the flowers and the red areas outside the center medallions have been machine stitched; and two sections on the right and a part of a third have the appliques machine stitched in places; the rest have been hand sewn. This probably suggests two separate workers; or, it could signify the acquiring of a new sewing machine and eagerness to "show it off."

Photo # 29 Courtesy Ruth Margarida, Jasper, Indiana

Photo # 30 Courtesy Mrs. Frank Lovell, Versailles, Ky.

Photo # 31 Courtesy Bill and Bunny Nolt, Worthington, Ohio

Photo # 32 Courtesy Dr. John Caton, Frankfort, Ky.

Photo # 33

Design: Four Point Feathered Star
Type: Patchwork
Size: 78″ x 93″
Maker: Margaret Beshear Patterson, Hardin County, Kentucky
Date: c. 1865
Condition: Excellent
Quilting: Large, "waffle"-centered medallions
Value: $800.00 - $1,100.00

Comments: The design and colors used are typical of this time period.

Photo # 34

Design: Solomon's Temple Variation
Type: Patchwork
Size: 80″ x 87″
Maker: N. H. Martin, Ashland City, Tennessee
Date: March 29, 1869
Condition: Excellent
Quilting: Diamonds and double lines; diamonds in 10 stitches per inch; double line borders in brown thread, 7-8 stitches per inch
Value: $1,250.00 - $1,800.00

Comments: This design prefaces the large, graphic, geometric designs seen in the 1880's and 1890's. The brown border fabric has tiny swastika designs.

Photo # 35

Design: Drunkard's Path
Type: Patchwork
Size: 76″ x 78″
Maker: Unknown, from Lima, Ohio
Date: c. 1870
Condition: Purple fading to brown; some fuzzing of binding
Quilting: Excellent; diamond and outline; 10-12 stitches per inch
Value: $450.00 - $750.00

Photo # 36

Design: Tree of Life
Type: Patchwork
Size: 78″ x 92″
Maker: Unknown; Larue County, Kentucky
Date: c. 1870
Condition: Good
Quilting: Good; mostly straight line
Value: $500.00 - $750.00

Comments: Material is a purple sprigged fabric.

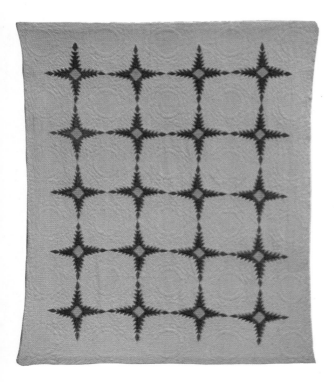

Photo # 33 Courtesy Mrs. Hollis Williams, Hodgensville, Ky.

Photo # 34

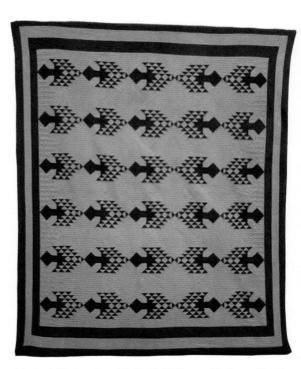

Photo # 35

Photo # 36 Courtesy Hollis P. Williams, Hodgenville, Ky.

1850 - 1874

Photo # 37, 38

Design: Whole cloth
Type: Whole cloth
Size: 68″ x 85″
Maker: Unknown; Ohio
Date: c. 1870?
Condition: Average
Quilting: Tied
Value: $125.00 - $175.00

Comments: The style of English quilts is to make them of "whole cloth", merely sewing appropriate lengths and sizes of fabrics together to make a covering.

This fabric is tissue thin, the kind you can "read the Bible through" and with those giant pictures of the hunt scene with the lady riding side saddle, in brown and red, no less, I WANT to say the fabric is 1830's at least. However, the quilt is machine sewn, so it's doubtful it was put together before the 1870's. The batting is wool. The paisley side was meant to be the "show" side. That extra strip of "V" patterned fabric in moss, yellow and pink (also thin, and very 1825-ish) was added to protect the head edge of the quilt.

The reason I'm so "bent" on the fabrics being earlier is because I know there was a "style" back then of fabrics being so thin that ladies were forced to wear "pantalettes" beneath their dresses and petticoats to keep from (horrors!) having the silhouette of their "limbs" seen. (These were our first "trousers," girls!) Everything "fits" the 1825-1840 time except that machine stitching! It's a silly fabric to use in a quilt. Maybe the lady bought it and "chickened out" of using it in a dress and then later made it into a comfort?

I thought it worth buying to show you an English way of making quilts. This doesn't mean the quilt was made in England, merely that it was made in the English way.

Photo # 39

Design: Castle Wall
Type: Patchwork "Presentation" Quilt
Size: 71″ x 81″
Maker: Blocks by various people named Smith, Cook, Cain, Fry and Martin
Date: March 4, 1875; presented to "M. J. Sheek" or "Sheer"
Condition: Generally good; unwashed, but stained as from roof leak
Quilting: Triple line
Value: $450.00 - $650.00

Comments: The value of this quilt is much diminished by the staining which might be removed with washing; but so might the names, dating and verse which reads in part as follows: "May thy joys be many — Cares be few — Smooth be ___ ___ ___ road — Shall ___ ___ ___ — And Heaven's Richest Blessings ever shine — Brighter in thee."

Novice quilters please take note of how very different many of these blocks look despite having the same Castle Wall design in all.

The odd blue color of the sashing material is typical of the 1870's and 1880's.

Photo # 40

Design: Prince's Feather (Princess Feather, Star and Plume)
Type: Applique
Size: 82″ x 96″
Maker: Grandmother of Mrs. Ann O'Brien
Date: c. 1870's
Condition: Excellent
Quilting: Stippled or 1/8″ apart; standing leaves or tracks throughout
Value: $3,000.00 - $4,000.00

Comments: This quilt pattern had been popular since the 1830's, but interest was rekindled in the early 1870's, possibly due to national coverage of the great buffalo hunt being carried on in the West by the Grand Duke Alexis of Russia, guest of the renowned buffalo hunter Bill Cody. It was reported that the imagination of the entire nation was taken by the event and there was much talk of the Duke and nobility in general.

Photo # 37, 38

Photo # 39

Photo # 40 Courtesy Lois's Antiques, Hodgenville, Ky.

Photo # 41

Design: **Double Peony with Starburst Lillies**
Type: Patchwork
Size: 74½″ x 98½″
Maker: Unknown; Illinois
Date: c. 1880
Condition: Good
Quilting: Average; triple line and shell; 8 stitches per inch
Value: $850.00 - $1,250.00

Comments: The overall design of this quilt is doubtless "original"; but, with me, at least, it "works". The rail fence (zigzag, rick-rack, streak of lightning) border treatment is typical of the 1880's though it has been seen in quilts dated before 1850 and after 1930.

Photo # 42

Design: **English Rose Variation**
Type: Applique
Size: 78¼″ x 92½″
Maker: Unknown; Harrison County, Kentucky
Date: c. 1880
Condition: Good; one binding fray; one flower fray; some tiny staining
Quilting: Diagonal lines, 3/8″ apart; stitching extremely even
Value: $950.00 - $1,450.00

Comments: Not everyone will like this busy applique with its overall "folk" look. However, Mrs. Lovell considered it quite a "find" particularly in view of the fact that someone before her turned it down because they thought it was machine stitched. On close examination, the quilt proves hand done, but with stitching so even it appears machine done! Think of it, quilters! This lady achieved the much-sought perfection of EVEN STITCHES only to have her work "rejected!" What irony!

Photo # 41 Courtesy Rod Lich and Susan Parrett, ''Folkways'', Georgetown, Ind.

Photo # 42 Courtesy of Mrs. Frank Lovell, Versailles, Ky.

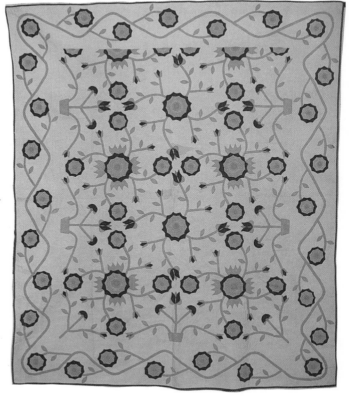

Photo # 43

Design: Star of Four Points
Type: Patchwork; Political
Size: 86″ x 86″
Maker: Unknown
Date: c. 1880
Condition: Excellent; colors still exceptionally vivid
Quilting: Fine; but secondary to the vivid design
Value: $4,500.00 - $5,500.00

Comments: The center of the quilt is a commemorative bandana honoring James A. Garfield (who was president from March 4, 1881 until September 19, 1881, when he died of blood poisoning from an assassin's bullet) and Chester Alan Arthur, his vice presidential running mate, who subsequently became President from September 20, 1881, until March 3, 1885.

Collectors are ever watchful for quilts with "commentary" on the times in which they were made. This is an outstanding example of one with political significance. The value of this quilt is enhanced, unfortunately, by the drama surrounding the 20th President's death. It is also helped by the bold, geometric design and the skill with which the various colors of fabrics were assembled.

There are various "thoughts" surrounding the quilt, one being that it was made during the campaign as a show of Republican support; one, that it was made directly after Garfield was killed, as a "memorial". The "star" design, of course, would fit either event. I tend to believe the bright colors lend credence to the first belief. On the other hand, if a woman made this, it may have been her not-so-subtle way of influencing her husband's vote in the election since she, as yet, had no vote--a politics of the bedroom, so to speak!

Photo # 44

Design: American Flag
Type: Patchwork with embroidery; Political
Size: 84″ x 84″
Maker: Unknown
Date: December 23, 1876 - December 23, 1882
Condition: Excellent
Value: $4,500.00 - $5,500.00

Comments: Political quilts, particularly flag and eagle-festooned ones that can be related to the country's Centennial celebration in 1876, are eagerly sought by serious collectors. Greater demand in any field of collectibles results in high prices for said items; and generally speaking, these items with built-in demand have the most potential as "investments."

The embroidery work on the center white cross sashing includes a cameo picture of Abraham Lincoln; his dates directly above that; some 1869 dates beside the cities of Franklin and Nashville, Tennnessee; some military battalion names and numbers; and the names of Mark L. Quardo (?), December 23, 1876, followed by "presented by Fannie Q., Dec. 23rd, 1882." One gets the impression that Fannie "gifted" the idea or top to Mark in 1876 as a means of recording his military service record and then presented him with the "fait accompli" in 1882. Possibly she anticipated his career being somewhat more glorious than it was, owning to the amount of space she reserved to embroider.

Photo # 43 Courtesy Shelly Zegart's Quilts, Louisville, Ky.

Photo # 44 Courtesy Shelly Zegart's Quilts, Louisville, Ky.

1875 - 1899

Photo # 45

Design: Urn of Roses (similar to Kentucky Flower Pot)
Type: Applique
Size: 74" x 77"
Maker: Unknown; Lebanon, Tennessee
Date: c. 1885
Condition: Average; some stains which may or may not remove when washed
Quilting: Shell
Value: $450.00 - $600.00

Comments: Machine appliqued in contrasting thread so you'd be certain to notice the machine stitching. Three piece backing. There is an "obvious flaw." One of the secondary center applique designs has been switched with one near the border.

Photo # 46

Design: Urn of (Le Moyne) Star Lillies
Type: Applique and patchwork
Size: 85" x 85"
Maker: Unknown; Shelbyville, Indiana
Date: c. 1885
Condition: Average; some stains
Quilting: Diamonds; average, 8 stitches per inch
Value: $500.00 - $750.00

Comments: There is an interesting border treatment on this quilt in that the winding vine encompasses only two sides of the quilt; the other sides are made up of carefully placed, free-standing blossoms. Cotton seed batting.

Photo # 47

Design: Star of Chamblie (antique French design) **with a Star and Wreath center**
Type: Patchwork
Size: 89" x 89"
Maker: Unknown; Jasper, Indiana
Date: c. 1883
Condition: Excellent
Quilting: Below average; inch squares, large stitches
Value: $950.00 - $1,450.00

Comments: What this quilter lacked in quilting skills, she made up in color and and design. She has combined two patterns into a skillful whole. You can "feel" the German influence behind the combination of colors. It's a visual delight!

Photo # 48

Design: Starburst with Circled Star accents
Type: Patchwork
Size: 74" x 76"
Maker: Unknown; Indiana
Date: c. 1890
Condition: Average plus; some stains
Quilting: Outline; diamonds and straight lines (inch apart) border quilting
Value: $500.00 - $750.00

Photo # 45

Photo # 46 Courtesy Rick Norton, Noblesville, Ind.

Photo # 47 Courtesy Ruth Margarida, Jasper, Ind.

Photo # 48 Courtesy Rod Lich and
Susan Parrett, Georgetown, Ind.

Photo # 49

Design: Prairie Flower (Rose Tree, Missouri Rose)
Sawtooth (Bear's Tooth) border; some confusion at the outside corner joints
Type: Applique and patchwork
Size: 73" x 80"
Maker: Unknown; from Ohio
Date: c. 1880
Condition: Good
Quilting: Average; ½"-¾" diamonds, leaf and circles in boundary, 8 stitches per inch
Value: $750.00 - $1,000.00

Comments: This is an older design and put together in four huge blocks as was characteristic of older quilts. However, due to its smaller size, the larger area between lines of quilting, the circle and leaf motifs and the leaves of that interesting shade of blue, I tend to believe this was made near the latter end of the applique-quilting furor.

Photo # 50

Design: Le Moyne Star
Type: Patchwork
Size: 63½" x 81"
Maker: Unknown; from Ohio
Date: c. 1878
Condition: Average-minus; some fading and wear
Quilting: Medallions in plain centers
Value: $150.00 - $225.00

Comments: Fabrics include a sprigged pink having a square pink "flower" and a sprigged green "morning glory" motif against a brown ground; one of the stars has a lighter blue ground than the navy backed "centennial" star. I've seen the lighter ground print in a museum quilt dated as 1837, evidence that this fabric may have been saved for quite some time, something not at all unusual.

I'm of the opinion that COLORS can help you date quilts equally well as the fabrics themselves. Many of the fabric designs have been repeated by the manufacturing companies again and again. Ely Mfg. Co. was kind enough to send me a chart of eighteen prints that have been in their line since its inception in 1878. Thus, **designs** which have proven popular with the buying public often have great longevity.

Photo # 51

Design: Old Sawtooth
Type: Patchwork
Size: 73" x 76"
Date: c. 1880
Condition: Average-minus; border very frayed
Quilting: Average; squares and diagonal lines ½" to ¾" apart; knots showing on back
Value: $150.00 - $200.00

Photo # 52

Design: Unknown; (Variation of Pointing Star)
Type: Patchwork (Utilitarian)
Size: 86" x 88"
Maker: Mrs. Patterson (Quaker), Chesterhill, Ohio
Date: c. 1885
Condition: Average-minus; five triangles deteriorating
Quilting: Average; outline, cable border
Value: $200.00 - $250.00

Comments: This quilt is a mine of fabrics from this time frame, small sprigs, dark background checks, stars, poseys, older "shirting" materials (white with very tiny dots, sprigs, swirls and leaves), and black and white prints of varying designs. The backing is a black and white fabric that has a double image "hairpin" motif. A further indication of its Victorian roots lies in the geometric type pattern chosen. Notice the sawtooth inner border.

Photo # 49 Courtesy Leo and Mary K. Walter
Stagecoach Antiques, Akron, Ohio

Photo # 50

Photo # 51 Courtesy Leo Walter, Stagecoach Antiques,
Akron, Ohio

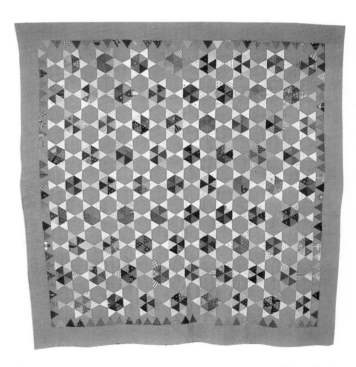

Photo # 52

Photo # 53

Design: **Crazy Patch** with elaborate embroidery and ribbon work
Type: Patchwork
Size: 73″ x 76″
Maker: Unknown; Kansas
Date: c. 1885
Condition: Average; a couple of silk fabrics missing
Quilting: Backing quilted separately and now ''lumped''
Value: $225.00 - $300.00

Comments: This quilt is made mostly of velvet patches which have withstood the passage of time. Quilts made from silks have often fallen to pieces. Velvet crazy quilts are thought to be good investments at this time since they are still relatively inexpensive, having been lumped together with the fragmented silk quilts.

Midwestern influence is seen in the embroidered wheat stem and the scythe. Other emblems are more typical, namely the Sunbonnet, bird, dog, butterfly, owl, anchor, and the flower strewn initials (C.N. - J.H. - A.N.). The flowers have been made from ribbon tape, however, rather than embroidery. Ribbon work was popular then.

Photo # 54

Design: **Nine Block Crazy**
Type: Patchwork
Size: 71″ x 73″
Maker: Lula Weaver
Date: 1882
Condition: Good; some deterioration of the silks
Quilting: Border carefully machine quilted in 5/8″ squares
Value: $250.00 - $400.00

Comments: Fabrics are velvet, silks, satin brocade and a rust colored cotton backing. The cream satin material was from her wedding dress. The flowers are painted. Other designs worked into the craziness include a fan, a velvet shoe, a horse shoe and a quarter moon.

Photo # 55

Design: **Crazy Patch Fan**
Type: Patchwork
Size: 60½″ x 72″
Maker: Unknown; Kansas
Condition: Average; wire worked leaves coming loose; silk backing deteriorating
Quilting: Wool batting attached to the backing fabric by machine, but held in place at center via tiny red ribbons
Value: $250.00 - $400.00

Comments: The border of this is done in wire worked leaves (a material much like pipe cleaners that was used in sundry ways in Victorian handwork.)

Photo # 56

Design: **Thirty Block Crazy**
Type: Patchwork
Size: 67″ x 82″
Maker: Attributed to Maude Knogel family, Clarksville, Indiana
Date: 1887
Condition: Average; some silk deterioration
Quilting: None
Value: $250.00 - $400.00

Comments: Most interest in this quilt is generated by the treatment of the velvet border. Embroidery subjects include birds, flowers, knife, fork, scissors, dog, vase, Sunbonnets, cross, heart, shoes, horse shoes, leaves, butterflies, and chickens, all of which probably had some special ''meaning'' to the people of that day.

Photo # 53

Photo # 54
Courtesy Mr. and Mrs. James Gay,
Versailles, Ky.

Photo # 55 Courtesy Daisey Swanner, Conroe, Texas

Photo # 56

Photo # 57

Design: **Log Cabin** - Barn Raising Configuration
Type: Patchwork
Size: 70½" x 80"
Maker: Barbara Lehmann Swiss, Monroe County, Ohio
Date: c. 1885
Condition: Excellent; was only used on Sunday's and "special" occasions
Quilting: None
Value: $500.00 - $900.00

Comments: The quilt has the maker's mark of "Five Daisies" embroidered at one corner. Ms. Swiss has given a unique border treatment of individual log blocks. She was of a persuasion known as "Coffee Potters," who were known to be thrifty and saving in the extreme. Quilts were allowed only to be made from scraps, making one appreciate the beauty of this one all the more.

Photo # 58

Design: **Spring Beauty** (Crimson Rambler)
Type: Patchwork
Size: 72" x 79"
Maker: Mrs. John Schofield (Quaker), Ohio
Date: c. 1890
Condition: Some staining
Quilting: Double line; single cable in inner border ribbon
Value: $300.00 - $400.00

Photo # 59

Design: **Starburst** (Sunburst)
Type: Patchwork
Size: 65" x 83"
Maker: Margaret Susan Frain Rogers (at age 11)
Date: 1887
Condition: Large areas of stains
Quilting: Squares; 6 even stitches per inch
Value: $150.00 - $200.00

Comments: It was not unusual for young girls to make quilts. Indeed, a young lady was supposed to have had a dozen to her credit, reserving the thirteenth as her "Wedding Quilt."

Quilting of the Starburst in tiny, ¾" diamonds is indicative of a trend toward miniaturization that had its roots here. Up until the 1870's, a quilt was judged on how many spools of thread it took to quilt it, the idea being, the more thread used, the better the quilt.

From the 1880's until the early 1940's, the more PIECES you could get into a quilt, the better. One famous quilt is known to have more than 87,000 pieces in it.

Photo # 60

Design: **Double X**
Type: Patchwork
Size: 69" x 83"
Maker: Unknown; Ohio
Date: c. 1885
Condition: Some browns deteriorating
Quilting: Diagonal line
Value: $250.00 - $325.00

Comments: This quilt needs laundering, but I dare not attempt it until I can sew netting over a couple of triangles that are very fragile looking. After this procedure is done, I can soak it using a mild soap and rinse it thoroughly. Then, the quilt can be gently rolled free of water, rolled in a blanket to further remove water and then laid out on some tall grass (out of the sun) to dry. Hanging a wet quilt may damage it. The combination of ozone rays and chlorophyll-laden grass is a natural bleaching process that will further brighten the colors of the quilt; sunlight would, of course, fade them. Most people choose to soak quilts in their bath tubs. Newer quilts can be washed in machines as long as they aren't spun dry. Spinning breaks the quilting threads.

Photo # 57 Courtesy of Helen Marshall, Doylestown, Ohio

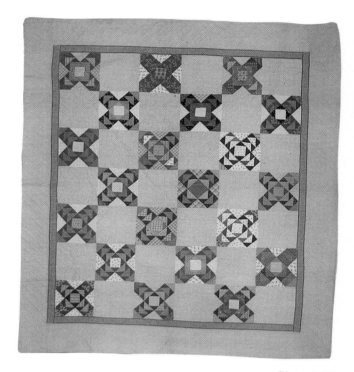

Photo # 58

Photo # 59 Courtesy of Katherine Hughes, Louisville, Ky.

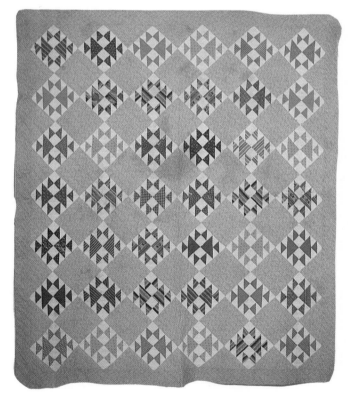

Photo # 60

Photo # 61

Design: Spools
Type: Patchwork, Presentation
Size: 68″ x 82″
Makers: Anna Garrday, Lela Cox, Becky Chappel, Ola Cox and Elsie Wall; Carrolton, Georgia
Date: 1888
Condition: Average; some stains
Quilting: ¼″ circles
Value: $350.00 - $500.00

Comments: This quilt has probably never been washed so the staining might remove, as might the inked-in names and date. Notice the swastika motif achieved through the arrangement of the spools.

Photo # 62

Design: Album Patch
Type: Patchwork
Size: 74½″ x 81½″
Maker: Unknown; Ohio
Date: c. 1885
Condition: Unused
Quilting: Large diamonds and triple line
Value: $175.00 - $250.00

Comments: The pattern was often used in friendship quilts (without the center block in colored fabric.) The blue patches are of the fabric being referred to as the ''Centennial Star'' (which simply means it was introduced for the Centennial, not that it wasn't made for several years after that.) The backing is a cheap, cheese cloth-appearing fabric that was often used as quilt backing. My grandmother remembers it being called ''quilt lining.'' To a Kentuckian, it looks rather like tobacco plant bed canvas.

Photo # 63

Design: Star Within A Star (Virginia Star; Bright Morning Star)
Type: Patchwork
Size: 66″ x 70″
Maker: Grandmother, ''Mote'' Durbin, Estill County, Kentucky
Date: c. 1888
Condition: Average; some fabric deterioration
Quilting: Outline; machine edging
Value: $225.00 - $300.00

Comments: Notice the vivid blue which is often used in quilts of this date. Note also how different the same design looks throughout the quilt.

Photo # 64

Design: Rainbow Stars
Type: Patchwork
Size: 69½″ x 86½″
Date: c. 1890
Condition: Average
Quilting: Giant circles
Value: $150.00 - $225.00

Comments: All of the star patterns are ''there''; the maker just turned one edge down due to the shortness of her backing material. There is an extra pink binding on one side; presumably she ran out of that, also. The backing of this quilt has been dyed with walnut hulls, turning it a rich, dark brown. This quilt fairly shouts ''country''; yet even with its faults, it conveys warmth and good cheer.

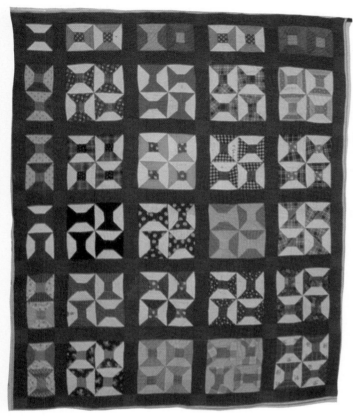

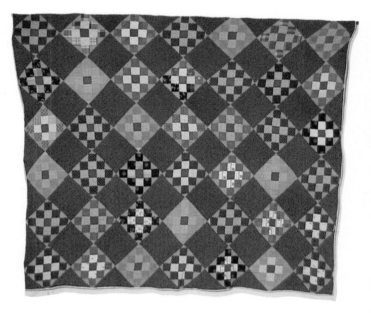

Photo # 61

Photo # 62

Photo # 63 Courtesy Mr. and Mrs. Maurice Rice,
Lexington, Ky.

Photo # 64 From Central Kentucky Antique Mall,
Georgetown, Ky.

1875 - 1899

Photo # 65

Design: **Shoofly II**
Type: Patchwork
Date: c. 1885
Condition: Poor; one square shredded
Quilting: Squares
Value: $125.00 - $250.00

Photo # 66

Design: **Indiana Puzzle** (Virginia Reel, square center) (Snail Trail, Monkey Wrench - 4 triangle center)
Type: Patchwork
Size: 73″ x 86″
Date: c. 1885
Condition: Excellent
Quilting: Outline; cable stitched borders
Value: $600.00 - $800.00

Comments: Backing is a printed cotton with a zigzag motif.

Photo # 67

Design: **Lone Star** (Star of Bethlehem)
Type: Patchwork
Size: 81½″ x 83″
Maker: Unknown; estate of E. Simonton, Youngstown, Ohio
Date: c. 1890
Condition: Average; silk backing is deteriorating (good top; poor backing)
Quilting: Outline and large feathered medallions at the corners
Value: $350.00 - $500.00

Comments: This quilt has been given some "crazy" quilt treatment in that there is briar stitching (embroidery) on each of the diamonds! This came from the estate of a lady who played the organ accompaniment to silent movies.

Photo # 68

Design: **Crazy Patch**
Type: Patchwork and Painted Flowers
Size: 79″ x 90½″
Maker: Sally Crowder Baldwin
Date: c. 1890
Condition: Good
Quilting: Tied, feather stitching
Value: $175.00 - $275.00

Comments: This quilt has painted flowers which was another way of decorating crazy quilts during this time. It's made of silks, satins, wools and velvet fabrics. One interesting patch is a "Stockport England" hat patch in gold. They wasted nothing then, not even hat linings.

Photo # 65 Courtesy Mrs. Frank Lovell, Versailles, Ky.

Photo # 66 Courtesy Rod Lich and Susan Parrett,
"Folkways", Georgetown, Ind.

Photo # 67 Courtesy Mr. and Mrs. Parke Bloyer, Poland, Ohio

Photo # 68 Courtesy Mr. and Mrs. W. C. Rose, Owenton, Ky.

1875 - 1899

Photo # 69

Design: **Garden Maze** (Tangled Garter)
Type: Patchwork
Maker: Unknown: Ohio
Date: c. 1890
Condition: Fragile
Value: $60.00 - $75.00

Photo # 70

Design: **Album Patch**
Type: Patchwork
Size: 76″ x 78″
Maker: Daughter of feed store owner (Miss Reed?), Marietta, Ohio
Date: c. 1890
Condition: Average; some fading
Quilting: Triple line, 8 stitches per inch
Value: $250.00 - $350.00

Comments: This is an excellent example of a ''feed sack'' backed quilt. Many people used their sacking fabrics in this manner, though often they dyed them or patched over the brand names in an effort to disguise the fact. This lady took pride in her father's business and made no effort to hide the fact that she used their sacks as backing for her quilts! This particular sacking reads as follows: ''Warings Fertilizers - Guaranteed Analysis - Wm. J. Reed, Agent - Marietta, Ohio - Uniform in Quality - Quick in their Action - Lasting in their results - Manufactured by the Waring Mfg. Co., Colora, Md.''

In the first years of collecting, many collectors rejected any ''feed sack'' quilt. Of late, there's a quiet movement to gather these up as specific types which are representative of a certain block of quilting work carried on by country quilters from the 1890's to the 1940's. In other words, the back of this quilt is almost as good as the front; and the time may come when it's better!

Photo # 71

Design: **Ocean Wave**
Type: Patchwork
Size: 68″ x 74″
Date: c. 1890
Condition: Good; crisp feel of disuse
Quilting: Double edged shell
Value: $375.00 - $525.00

Comments: This quilt has a self edge (back turned over front) which has been machine stitched. The fabrics are shirtings, Centennial Stars, pink and lavendar springs, and a plain pink which resembles denim fabric, though not that heavy.

Ocean Wave pattern has particular appeal to collectors because of its clean, geometric lines; it's very graphic, which was exactly the reason the pattern appealed to the Victorian quilter.

Photo # 72

Design: **Rolling Rainbow Stars** with variation of Rolling Star insets
Type: Patchwork
Size: 73″ x 81½″
Maker: Unknown; Fayette County, Kentucky
Date: c. 1890
Condition: Average-minus; fabrics missing; small stains; rebound
Quilting: Small squares
Value: $150.00 - $250.00

Comments: This quilt was made during the influence of miniaturization. The stars are made of ¾″ diamond patches. Dotted ''shirting'' and sprigged pink are the main fabrics used. Because of its problems, many serious collectors would pass buying it. Yet, with some small repairs (IN PERIOD FABRICS), this quilt could be a delight for years to come. It has a marvelous design, even having the half design to fit over the pillows! It has an ''obvious flaw'' patch in the glaring yellow star; and it has an abundance of those marvelous 100-year-old prints!

Photo # 69 Courtesy Mr. and Mrs. Robert Marshall, Doylestown, Ohio

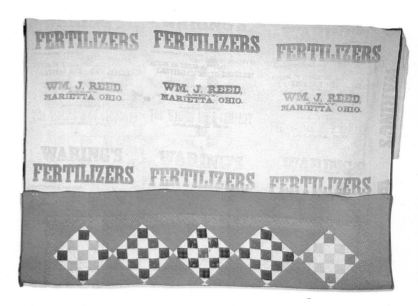

FERTILIZERS FERTILIZERS FERTILIZERS

WM. J. REED, MARIETTA OHIO.   WM. J. REED, MARIETTA OHIO.   WM. J. REED MARIETTA OHIO.

WARING'S FERTILIZERS   WARING'S FERTILIZERS   WARING'S FERTILIZERS

Photo # 70

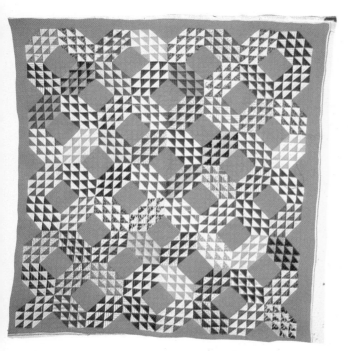

Photo # 71

Photo # 72 Courtesy of Ms. Lois Florence, Arlington, Va.

51

1875 - 1899

Photo # 73

Design: Butterfly at Crossroads
Type: Patchwork
Size: 56″ x 72″
Maker: Unknown; Indiana
Date: c. 1890
Condition: Average
Quilting: Small squares
Value: $150.00 - $225.00

Photo # 74

Design: Whirlwind
Type: Patchwork
Size: 84″ x 85½″
Maker: Unknown; Evansville, Indiana
Date: c. 1885
Condition: Good
Quilting: Diamonds
Value: $500.00 - $750.00

Photo # 75

Design: Unknown (type of Pineapple Cross with Roses or Oak Leaves)
Type: Applique
Date: April 10, 1891
Condition: Good; some faint staining
Quilting: Excellent; diamonds; large "waffle" centered, double feather-edged medallions
Value: $1,000.00 - $1,400.00

Comments: Red and tan appliques often date around 1890 indicating it was a "trend" at that time. I saw one sell very quickly at a flea market (dated 1892) for $500.00. It was badly stained; but the buyer was willing to gamble the stains would remove.
    The maker of this example included the "obvious flaw", pink petals in one of the "rose" appliques.

Photo # 76

Design: Unknown, possibly original
Type: Applique - Utilitarian
Size: 64½″ x 76″
Date: c. 1890
Condition: Good
Quilting: Outline at ½″ intervals; 3 to 4 stitches per inch
Value: $350.00 - $450.00

Comments: The "magic" of this quilt lies in its extremely interesting design!
In it, the designer managed to achieve balance, harmony and movement at the same time. There's a touch of pink in the border designs; and the backing is pink, also. The bigger appliques have been machine stitched.

Photo # 73

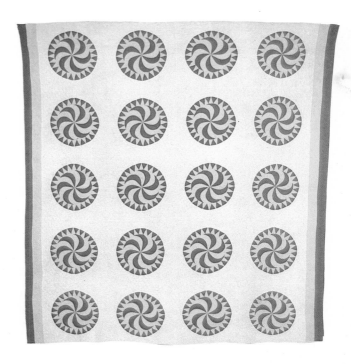

Photo # 74

Photo # 75 Courtesy Mrs. Frank Lovell, Versailles, Ky.

Photo # 76 Courtesy Mrs. Frank Lovell, Versailles, Ky.

Photo # 77

Design: Memory Block
Type: Patchwork
Size: 72″ x 84″
Maker: Unknown; Ohio
Date: c. 1890
Condition: Average
Quilting: Straight line, ½″
Value: $125.00 - $175.00

Photo # 78

Design: Double Saw Tooth Variation (extra pink block in center)
Type: Patchwork
Size: 64½″ x 79″
Maker: Unknown: Ohio
Date: c. 1890
Condition: Average; edge frayed, corner fading
Quilting: Double edged shell
Value: $225.00 - $275.00

Photo # 79

Design: Wild Goose Chase
Type: Patchwork
Size: 72″ x 77″
Maker: Unknown; Lancaster, Pennsylvania
Date: c. 1895
Condition: Good
Value: $250.00 - $350.00

Photo # 80

Design: Double Irish Chain (Chained Nine Patch)
Type: Patchwork
Size: 63″ x 72″
Maker: Carrie Lehmann
Date: c. 1890
Condition: Average; some brown fabric deterioration
Quilting: Diamonds, ¼″
Value: $300.00 - $425.00

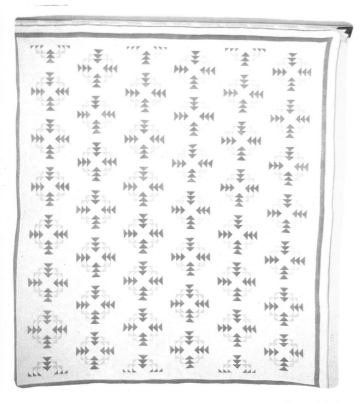

Photo # 77

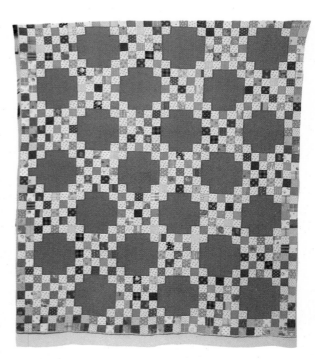

Photo # 78

Photo # 79 Courtesy Bill and Bunny Nolt, Worthington, Ohio

Photo # 80 Courtesy of Helen Marshall, Doylestown, Ohio

Photo # 81

Design: **Lone Star** (Star of Bethlehem)
Type: Patchwork and Applique
Size: 84″ x 85″
Maker: Unknown; Iowa
Date: c. 1890
Condition: Excellent
Quilting: Outline
Value: $1,300.00 - $1,600.00

Comments: This quilt shows a German influence in the cheerful colors used and the flower appliques. The edges have been machine bound and the background material is tiny "shirting" print.

Notice that two sides have an extra row of fabric causing the symmetry of the quilt to be off slightly. Also, some of the corners in the border treatments are mis-matched. However, as you can see, even with these flaws, the quilt is still a delight!

Photo # 82

Design: **Log Cabin** (Pictorial)
Type: Patchwork, wool and cotton
Maker: Unknown; Syracuse, New York
Date: c. 1890
Condition: Average; some moth damage; repaired
Quilting: Diagonal lines and in blocks
Value: Not available

Comments: This quilt has a lot going for it. It's unique, an original design. It's enhanced by the bright colors and the unusual combination of Wild Goose Chase and Sawtooth borders which give life and movement to an otherwise placid design. The Nine Patch corners were a stroke of genius, clearly setting boundaries to the "picture" and drawing it into a whole entity. This represents skilled, early textile design in a form practically unheard of in this time frame. Everyone else was into cubes and the latest pattern shown in *Godey's Ladies Book.* Yet, this quilter didn't totally abandon her geometric time frame. There is much that is geometric in rows of logs, windows, doors, sky, grass and border. It's an extraordinary piece of textile art!

The binding material is woven; the window panes were made by applying tiny strips of braid to the patch.

Photo # 81 Purchased from Joan Townsend,
Lebanon, Ohio

Photo # 82 Courtesy Rod Lich and Susan Parrett,
"Folkways", Georgetown, Ind.

Photo # 83

Design: Half Princess Feather/Half California Plume
Type: Applique
Size: 89″ x 93″
Maker: Attributed to Keller family, Pennsylvania to Hartford City, Indiana
Date: c. 1890
Condition: Excellent
Quilting: Inch squares, 9 stitches per inch
Value: $1,500.00 - $2,000.00

Comments: This was a wedding quilt. The swags, leaves and binding were dyed with a home-made dye made from brewing green leaves. There's an obvious flaw. The family believed this to be from the 1830's. The pattern may date from then and the quilt may have been copied from the older pattern since it was popular in the 1830's. However, the pink fabric in the "watermelon" swags matches exactly the pink in the Ocean Wave quilt; and the ground fabric isn't a proper weave to be 1830 as far as I'm concerned. Further, the quilting isn't close enough or of a proper design to be that old. Even so, the quilt is magnificent; and we shouldn't lose sight of that by quibbling over an extra half century date.

Photo # 84

Design: Lozenge
Type: Patchwork, wool
Size: 72″ x 81½″
Maker: Unknown; Western Kentucky (Mennonite?)
Date: c. 1890
Condition: Average; some moth damage
Quilting: Diagonal lines, ½″ apart
Value: $350.00 - $500.00

Comments: The design is unusual in that it has purposely been made to "travel" across the quilt. The colors are rich and striking, set into the moss green fabric. Someone suggested this might be Amish. I doubt that since it has only one border and the back fabric is a black and white print with a tiny pink rose on it. Amish aren't print-oriented.

Photo # 85

Design: Ocean Wave
Type: Patchwork
Size: 75½″ x 77½″
Maker: Unknown; Ohio
Date: c. 1895
Condition: Excellent; unwashed
Quilting: Diagonal lines, inch apart
Value: $500.00 - $750.00

Comments: The white fabrics are "shirting" dots and sprigs; the green is sprigged.

Photo # 83 Purchased from Alcorn Antiques, Centerville, Ind.

Photo # 84 Courtesy Anne Bugg, Wells Landing, Danville, Ky.

Photo # 85

1900 - 1924

Photo # 86

Design: **Geometric**
Type: Patchwork
Size: 81″ x 84″
Maker: Unknown; Wheeling, West Virginia
Date: c. 1890
Condition: Good
Quilting: Double line
Value: $1,200.00 - $1,800.00

Comments: Collectors value the unique and unusual and that which is representative of a certain period of time. This one fits all those criteria. The Victorian period saw great emphasis placed on geometric designs.

Photo # 87

Design: **Columbia Star Variation** (cube in center of star is unusual)
Type: Patchwork; Political
Size: 64″ x 86″
Date: c. 1898
Condition: Poor; faded and stretched from shape
Quilting: Double line ¼″ alternated with diagonal line 1″
Value: $250.00 - $350.00

Comments: Even though it's badly faded, this quilt is wonderful! The old calico prints and the unusual treatment of the Victorian design make it very special. It is machine bound and backed with "quilt lining" muslin.

Photo # 88

Design: **Lone Star or Texas Star** (Ohio and Variable Stars are cut like this but have an extra square in the center)
Type: Patchwork
Size: 93″ x 103″
Maker: Rose Miller Gump, Oklahoma
Date: 1904
Condition: Poor; edges badly frayed, some fabric missing
Quilting: Leaf motifs in white; shells, vine border
Value: $75.00 - $125.00; Intrinsic value -- priceless!

Comments: The fabric is blue with tiny white circles. The quilt is here because it deserves to be. This quilt was used during a prairie schooner trip from Oklahoma to the center of New Mexico and then back again to Ohio! It traveled 1,500 miles in use as cushioning against the rough wagon seat and as a bedroll beneath the wagon at night!

Photo # 89

Design: **Rainbow Stars**
Type: Patchwork
Size: 88″ x 88″
Maker: Unknown; Ohio
Date: c. 1905
Condition: Excellent
Quilting: Center medallions
Value: $300.00 - $425.00

Comments: This quilt is prettier than it appears in the photo. It is a "blue and white" combination that is being eagerly sought by collectors, particularly those in the mid-states.

Photo # 86 Courtesy Rod Lich and Susan Parret
"Folkways", Georgetown, Ind.

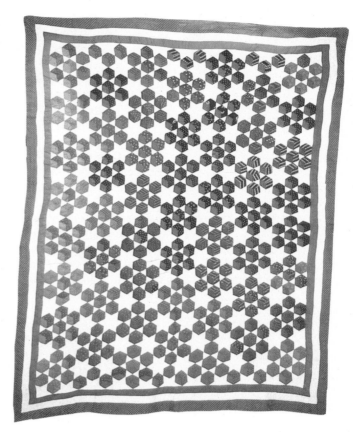

Photo # 87 Courtesy Mrs. Frank Lovell, Versailles, Ky.

Photo # 88 Courtesy Charles and Helen Dishong,
Akron, Ohio

Photo # 89 Courtesy Marcel Ulrich, McDonald, Ohio

Photo # 90

Design: Snowball
Type: Patchwork
Size: 66″ x 71″
Maker: Ida Cox
Date: December 25, 1902
Condition: Excellent
Quilting: Diamonds, flower medallions and cable
Value: $350.00 - $500.00

Comments: This is a family quilt with blocks containing all their names. As it happened, we saved the quilt from being damaged. The owner had just hung it on her son's bedroom wall (so he could get acquainted with his ''roots''), but had put it up with push pins which would have gathered moisture and rusted on the quilt.

Quilts should be hung like a painting. They should be attached to a backing ''canvas'' and framed by stretching the auxiliary fabric around the wooden frame. That way there is no stress on the edges of the quilt. Barring that, they can be attached to surfaces via velcro strips and hung. Three months a year is recommended hang-time for a quilt. After that, it should be stored out of the light for a period of rest. Never hang quilts in sunlight or spotlight them with bright lights since that will cause fading.

Photo # 91

Design: Young Man's Fancy (Goose in the Pond)
Type: Patchwork
Size: 66″ x 72″
Date: c. 1910
Condition: Average-minus; edges frayed
Quilting: Diagonal lines, 1¼″ apart
Value: $150.00 - $225.00

Photo # 92

Design: Rising Sun
Type: Patchwork
Size: 71″ x 87″
Maker: Unknown; Michigan
Date: c. 1900
Condition: Excellent
Quilting: Giant circles and cable edge
Value: $275.00 - $350.00

Comments: This is an old top that has been newly quilted, a practice that is more common now with the elevation of quilts from the bedroom to the Board Rooms as textile art. The batting is polyester which is ''puffier''; the quilting is wider apart; the edge treatment is a modern ''Prairie Points''; and the border fabrics, though a good blend, do not match those of the original top. There was no attempt made to ''disguise'' this quilt as old. That is not always the case. You have to learn to read textile ''signs'' as the old Indian tracker reads tracks.

Circular patterns, though harder to accomplish, seem to have been very popular with quilters from 1880 to 1900.

Photo # 93

Design: Old Maid's Puzzle
Type: Patchwork
Size: 61″ x 75″
Date: c. 1910
Condition: Average-plus
Quilting: Diagonal lines
Value: $275.00 - $375.00

Comments: This quilt has good graphics, good color combination (red and white is particularly attractive to collectors in the South), and it is small enough to hang or to use as a basis for enlarging.

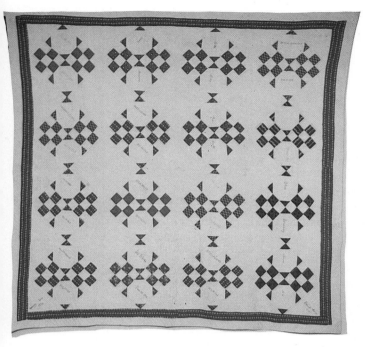

Photo # 90 Courtesy Becky Alexander, Uniontown, Ohio

Photo # 91

Photo # 92

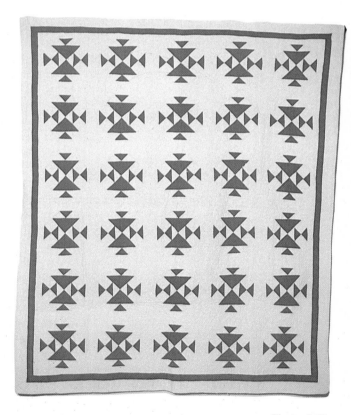

Photo # 93

1900 - 1924

Photo # 94

Design: **Pinwheels** (Old Crow, Crow's Foot, Kathy's Ramble, Sugar Bowl, Fan, Fan Mill, Fly and Fly Foot)
Type: Patchwork (Utilitarian)
Size: 79" x 90½"
Maker: Unknown; Ohio
Date: c. 1905
Condition: Excellent; like new, never washed; still has "sizing" or glazing on the fabric
Quilting: Below average; outline stitching with cable border; stitching of indifferent sizes
Value: $250.00 - $400.00

Comments: Collectors look for "crisp" quilts, or quilts that have had little or no use; unwashed quilts are considered extremely choice items! In fact, there are serious collectors who will purchase ONLY unwashed quilts. I find that extreme and unnecessarily limiting myself; but to each his own. I mention this to warn lady dealers (whose first thought is to take the quilt home and "wash it" before putting it out for sale) that if the quilt hasn't been washed before, (and hasn't been used to cover the chicken coop), it is better to leave it as is.

The fabrics in this are wonderful! Navy blues with tiny white designs; "shirting" fabrics of pink and white stripes; pink and purple sprigged flowers; and the backing is a special "treat" with "sign of the times", red and black tumbling blocks.

There is about a 25-year period (1885-1910) where rust colored fabrics were in vogue; the older rust colors have a "soft" look whereas the latter ones are brighter and of a more garish hue.

Photo # 95

Design: **Irish Chain**
Type: Patchwork
Size: 63" x 79"
Date: c. 1905
Condition: Average
Quilting: One inch straight line; large medallions in center
Value: $275.00 - $325.00

Photo # 96

Design: **Baby Blocks** (Cube Work; Tumbling Blocks)
Type: Patchwork
Size: 71" x 77½"
Date: c. 1905
Condition: Average; some fraying of materials
Quilting: Outline
Value: $350.00 - $500.00

Comments: This quilt has wonderful graphics and cube work quilts are particularly desirable to collectors. One in excellent condition could expect to bring $1,000.00 - $1,500.00

Photo # 97

Design: **Snowball**
Type: Patchwork
Size: 69½" x 71"
Date: c. 1910
Condition: Average; small gingham repair
Quilting: 1½" squares
Value: $250.00 - $375.00

Comments: Black center may have been an attempt at an "obvious flaw"; the backing fabric has a 1910 type lady in the design.

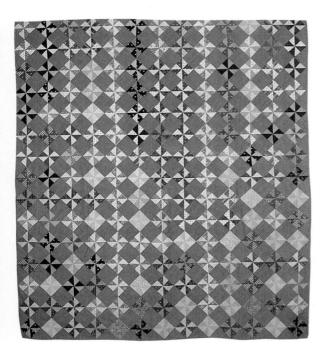

Photo # 94

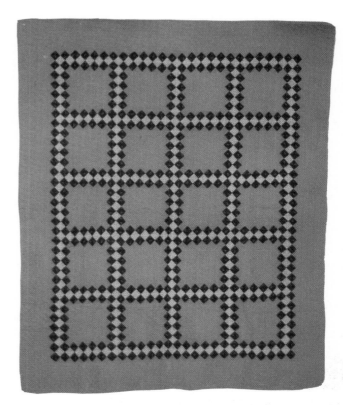

Photo # 95

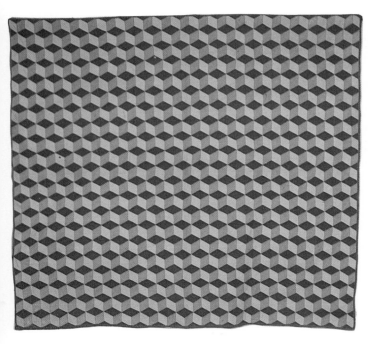

Photo # 96 Courtesy Mrs. Frank Lovell, Versailles, Ky.

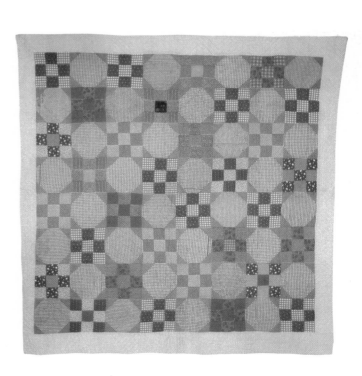

Photo # 97 Courtesy Mrs. Frank Lovell, Versailles, Ky.

Photo # 98

Design: Log Cabin (Court House Steps Configuration)
Type: Patchwork, wool
Size: 80″ x 84″
Maker: Unknown; Indiana
Date: 1907
Condition: Average
Quilting: Tied (comfort)
Value: $75.00 - $125.00

Comments: The interesting thing about this comfort, besides its being dated and made into the lesser seen Court House Steps arrangement, is that it's a quilt within a quilt. From a hole in the backing, you can see another patchwork quilt inside it. This was usually done when the first quilt was too worn to use; but rather than "waste" it, it was used as batting for a new quilt. It made this extremely heavy! (It wouldn't stay on the velcro strips and had to be held by hand at the photography studio; hence, the swag at the top!)

Photo # 99

Design: Chrysanthemum (Aster, Friendship Circle, Dresden Plate)
Type: Patchwork, wool and velvet
Size: 70″ x 81″
Date: c. 1908
Condition: Poor; very worn at the edges; but beautiful embroidery work still good
Value: $75.00 - $150.00

Comments: This pattern appeared in *Godey's Ladies Book* in 1898. With all the "crazy quilt" type stitching applied, and the fact that it was made in both wool and velvet seem to make it early 1900's. Too, there is an "obvious flaw" patch of lighter material. Embroidery work includes stitching around each petal, birds, butterflies, rooster, horse, leaves and fruit basket.

Photo # 100

Design: Hexagon (Ladies Art Company, 1898)
Type: Patchwork
Size: 76″ x 83″
Maker: Aleathea Baldwin
Date: c. 1908
Condition: Good
Quilting: Tied via embroidered "stars" at each hexagon point
Value: $350.00 - $500.00

Comments: Notice how the designs have been treated along the edges to make them work out properly.

Photo # 101

Design: Star
Type: Patchwork with Candlewicking
Size: 75″ x 79″
Maker: Unknown; Maine
Date: c. 1910
Condition: Body, good; ruffled edging very frayed
Quilting: None
Value: $150.00 - $250.00

Comments: The stars are formed via "sheered" candlewicking, causing them to puff up. Each patch is feather stitched.

Photo # 98

Photo # 99 Courtesy Carolyn Kugler, Livonia, Mich.

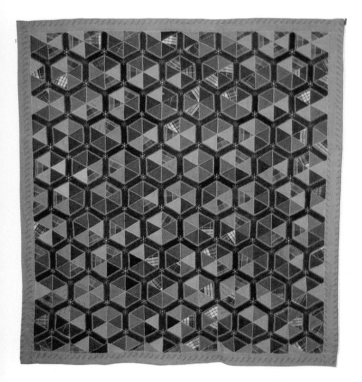

Photo # 100

Photo # 101

Photo # 102

Design: Sawtooth
Type: Patchwork
Size: 72″ x 82″
Maker: Mother of Mrs. Church, Wooster, Ohio
Date: c. 1910
Condition: Excellent
Quilting: Diamonds, ½″
Value: $275.00 - $350.00

Photo # 103

Design: **Variation of Whig, English or Tea Rose; or older Spice Pink pattern;** Pinwheel center belongs to none of the above and may be original
Type: Applique
Size: 64″ x 81″
Maker: Unknown; West Virginia
Date: c. 1910
Condition: Good
Quilting: Outline and hearts; very tiny applique stitches
Value: $350.00 - $500.00

Comments: The "boomerang" swags are unusual and one deliberately marches off the edge for an "obvious flaw". The "thorn" canes dividing the six squares are also unique and lend weight to the rose patterns mentioned above. The whole quilt has a marvelous primitive feel about it; and the tri-coloring couldn't be better!

Photo # 104

Design: Sampler
Type: Cross stitch
Size: 52″ x 86″
Maker: Unknown; Pennsylvania (Mennonite)
Date: c. 1910
Condition: Excellent
Value: $350.00 - $500.00

Comments: A big "push" in ladies' magazines from 1890 to the 1920's was the checked fabric cross stitch. These designs have been worked in 3-ply wool, an older technique. Notice the different border treatments of each design!

Photo # 105

Design: One Square
Type: Patchwork "Puff" Sofa Throw
Size: 46″ x 74″
Maker: Unknown; Frankfort, Kentucky
Date: c. 1915
Condition: Poor; several silks deteriorating
Quilting: None
Value: $50.00 - $75.00

Comments: The top patch of puff quilts are made larger than the bottom or backing, stuffed with cotton and then sewn to the backing fabric, creating a "puffed" look; hence the name. This technique is used mostly for pillows today; but in the late teens and early twenties, women's magazines touted this for sofa covers. The black satin fabrics in this are still good; but the silks are rapidly disappearing. The pink backing and ruffle are a rayon lining material. This could be restored.

Photo # 102 Courtesy Charles and Helen Dishong, Akron, Ohio

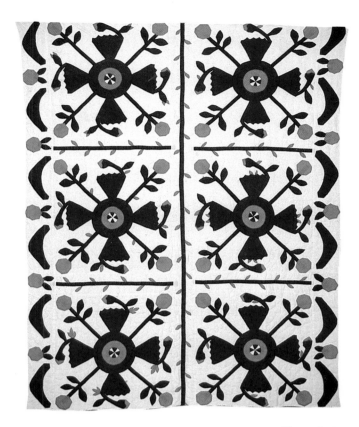

Photo # 103

Photo # 104 Purchased from Bruce and Charlotte Riddle,
Bardstown, Ky.

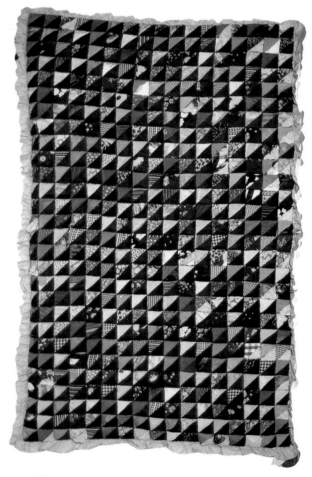

Photo # 105

Photo # 106

Design: **Sunbonnet**
Type: Embroidered Patchwork
Size: 73″ x 83″
Maker: Unknown; Flint, Michigan
Date: c. 1913
Condition: Good
Quilting: Fan with cable edging
Value: $250.00 - $325.00

Comments: There are 30 Sunbonnet designs depicting days of the week, months and seasons of the year. I've seen individual patches at the markets selling for $5.00 each. This quilt is enhanced by the Sawtooth border treatment.

Photo # 107

Design: **Sunbonnets, Kewpie Doll and Animals**
Type: Embroidered Patchwork
Size: 75¼″ x 84½″
Maker: Unknown; possibly a child; Pennsylvania
Date: c. 1918
Condition: Good
Quilting: Below average, 5½ stitches per inch
Value: $115.00 - $200.00

Comments: This quilt would delight a child and more than likely was put together by one. Symmetry isn't apparent with whole rows of elephants, cats and baskets. The quilt is machine edged. It has tulips quilted into the border, further identifying it with its Pennsylvania heritage.

Photo # 108

Design: **Wild Goose Chase**
Type: Patchwork
Size: 74½″ x 84″
Maker: Unknown; Terre Haute, Indiana
Date: c. 1915
Condition: Good
Quilting: Squares; 6 stitches to the inch
Value: $750.00 - $1,000.00

Photo # 109

Design: **Unknown**
Type: Patchwork
Size: 71″ x 85½″
Maker: Addie Remy, Chesterhill, Ohio
Date: 1918
Condition: Excellent; never washed
Quilting: Squares; inch apart; machine stitched edge
Value: $400.00 - $500.00

Comments: Modern quilters wouldn't allow the blue to show through the white as this does.

Photo # 106 Purchased from Country Catchin's, Lexington, Ky.

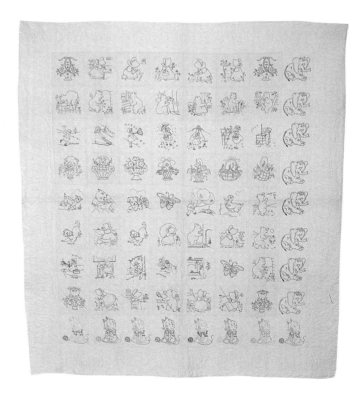

Photo # 107

Photo # 108 Courtesy Rod Lich and Susan Parrett,
"Folkways", Georgetown, Ind.

Photo # 109

Photo # 110

Design: Arrow Star (Variation in center circle)
Type: Patchwork, wool
Size: 71″ x 75″
Maker: Unknown; Northern Ohio
Date: c. 1915
Condition: Good
Quilting: Tied (Comfort); briar stitched
Value: $125.00 - $200.00

Comments: This comfort has a blue flannel backing, something very common to this time frame. It was made for warmth.

Photo # 111

Design: Crazy Patch Family Album
Type: Patchwork
Size: 60″ x 69″
Maker: Mary Alice Lawrence
Date: December 15, 1917
Condition: Excellent
Quilting: None; briar stitching
Value: $150.00 - $250.00

Comments: This quilt is covered with family names. The backing is blue roses and palm fronds, against a trellis background.

Photo # 112

Design: Grape Vine
Type: Whitework or Stuffed Work
Size: 84″ x 84″
Maker: "V. D. D."
Date: c. 1917
Condition: Excellent
Quilting: Outstanding
Value: $2,000.00 - $3,000.00

Comments: Whitework quilts, so common in the early 1800's (and before), all but died out around 1925. Until then, some mountain ladies were doing this sort of work as "cottage industries"; but machine made covers reduced the demand for their work.

Photo # 113

Design: The New Album
Type: Patchwork, wool and cotton
Size: 68″ x 89″
Maker: Rosa Mae Kemper Spicer (1874-1933)
Date: c. 1922
Condition: Average-plus; tiny moth damage
Quilting: Straight line, ½″ apart
Value: $250.00 - $350.00

Comments: Had I not written this book, I would never have known this quilt was anything "special". It just looks like a wool patchwork quilt with a flannel backing which I remember covering the "canning" in the upstairs bedroom of a mammoth roomed farm house. Those rooms got freezer cold in the winter; hence the protective covering for the summer's vegetable crop then neatly stored in glass canning jars.
   Hearing of my "project", my grandmother unearthed this from attic storage and proceeded to explain. "Momma made this when I first married. This was my dress; that's Momma's; and that checked material in the center was my grandmother's dress!" This quilt contains fabric from my great-great-grandmother's dress! That doesn't mean anything to you, I'm sure; but it means a lot to me! There IS an emotional bonding to "family" treasures, but only if their history is KNOWN. Do bother to write down what is known about the quilts in your family.

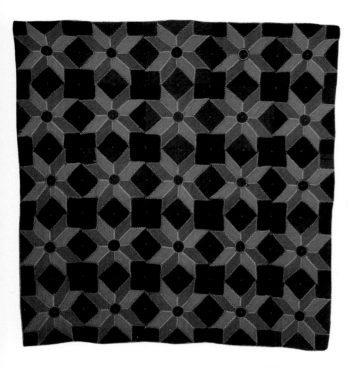

Photo # 110

Photo # 111 Courtesy Mr. and Mrs. Atwood Ayers, Owenton, Ky.

Photo # 112 Courtesy Shelly Zegart's Quilts, Louisville, Ky.

Photo # 113 Courtesy Marie Spicer Lucas, Lexington, Ky.

Photo # 114, 115, 116

Design: Flower Garden
Type: Patchwork
Size: 93″ x 104″
Maker: Caden Sisters, Lexington, Kentucky
Date: c. 1917
Condition: Good; a few silks deteriorating in the flower garden patches; some small spots on the gold satin backing quilt
Quilting: Good; fans, medallions, trapunto; 8 to 10 stitches per inch
Value: $2,500.00 - $3,000.00

Comments: This quilt is extraordinary! First, it was made for Charles Fisher (Fisher Body Works), of luxurious silks and satins and fabrics with spun gold threads. Second, it's a double quilt, the gold satin trapunto worked backing being an entirely separate quilt. Third, it was made by the Caden sisters of Lexington who ran a needlework shop in the Phoenix Hotel and enjoyed something of a national reputation for their superlative skills. Last, it has four corners and a center medallion worked in Petit Point, something that seems to have been a regional trend. (Besides this Fayette County example, another has been found in Bourbon County with Petit Point work.) Notice how the center design has been emphasized by the like color arrangement of the flowers in the first three rows.

The quilt is hurt by the fact it's a Flower Garden pattern, something dealers almost universally dismiss as being beneath their dignity to view. If anyone has a quilt in their home, it's likely to be a Flower Garden. I heard one dealer comment that he'd be happy if he never saw another one! It's also hurt by the fact that silks were used in its construction. Silk doesn't last like the poorer man's cotton fabrics. So, no matter how carefully it's handled, the silks are going to shred and fall away. Yet, even with these drawbacks, this is still a magnificent piece of textile art.

Photo # 114 and 115 Courtesy Mary V. Fisher, Lexington, Ky.

1900 - 1924

Photo # 117

Design: Basket
Type: Patchwork
Size: 70″ x 82″
Maker: Unknown; Tennessee
Date: c. 1920 (lady remembers 1910)
Condition: Excellent
Quilting: Outline; feathered medallions; hearts
Value: $450.00 - $600.00

Comments: Quilts quilted in hearts were often made for children or loved ones and/or made by people with "Dutch" origins. Collectors take particular notice of "hearts" in the quilting.

Photo # 118

Design: Necktie (Commonly Bow Tie)
Type: Patchwork
Maker: Mary Elizabeth Koeninger (1865-1932)
Date: 1919; Paradise, Texas
Condition: Good
Quilting: Outline; and sundry motifs
Value: $300.00 - $450.00

Comments: This quilt was made for her son "Edward" whose name is quilted into the lower edge of the quilt along with the date. It is said she made each of her six sons one exactly like this save for the names (wise mother; no hurt feelings over who got the "best" quilt).
There is a different motif quilted into each white block!
Necktie pattern is quite common; the quilting in this one raises it above the ordinary. Notice how the Tie has been emphasized by the diagonal line reaching from tip to tip.

Photo # 119

Design: Album
Type: Applique
Size: 79″ x 97″
Maker: Unknown; Delaware
Date: c. 1920
Condition: Excellent
Value: $2,200.00 - $3,000.00

Comments: An album quilt was something of an anachronism at this point; but here it is! The 1920's blues, greens and tans are in abundance. The designs appear original; particularly delightful is the squirrel upsetting the birds who are pictured in arched wing protest. The whole is beautifully tied by the winding leaves border. A nature lover made this quilt.

Photo # 117 From Uniontown House of Antiques, Uniontown, Ohio

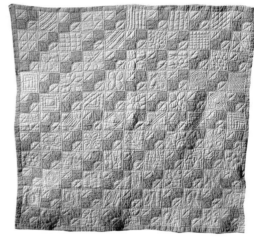

Photo # 118 Courtesy Mr. and Mrs. Dowden Koeninger, Sundown, Texas

Photo # 119 Courtesy Rod Lich and Susan Parrett, ''Folkways'', Georgetown, Ind.

Photo # 120

Design: **Jacob's Ladder** (Road to California in lighter colors)
Type: Patchwork
Size: 75″ x 89″
Maker: Addie Remy, Ohio
Date: c. 1922
Condition: Excellent; never used
Quilting: Diagonal lines; 1¼″ and squares
Value: $275.00 - $375.00

Photo # 121

Design: **Alphabet**
Type: Applique and Patchwork
Size: 73″ x 86″
Maker: Unknown; Dubois County, Indiana
Date: c. 1930
Condition: Excellent
Quilting: Outline, squares, waving lines
Value: $750.00 - $1,000.00

Comments: This is a special "type" quilt that many collectors hope to find for their collection.

Photo # 122

Design: **Patriotic Embroidered Sampler**
Type: Embroidered Patchwork
Size: 74″ x 88″
Maker: Unknown; Virginia
Date: c. 1930
Condition: Excellent
Quilting: Diamonds, ¾″
Value: $350.00 - $450.00

Comments: Designs included: 1492 Columbus Santa Maria; 1607 founding Jamestown; 1620 Pilgrims; 1775 Revere's Ride; 1777 Betsy Ross Flag; 1789 Washington; 1849 Gold Rush; 1854 Westward Movement; 1860 Lincoln; 1861 Civil War; 1863 Capitol Building; 1878 Indian. It has 13 eagles and 36 stars and was undoubtedly a kit.

Photo # 120

Photo # 121 Courtesy Ruth Margarida, Jasper, Ind.

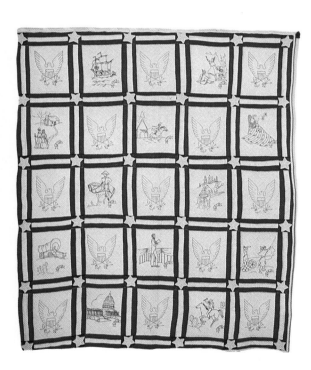

Photo # 122

79

1925 - 1949

Photo # 123

Design: North Carolina Lily (Mountain Lily; Fire Lily; Wood Lily; Meadow Lily; Prairie Lily; Noon Day Lily; Mariposa Lily)
Type: Patchwork
Size: 63″ x 81″
Maker: Mrs. Jenner, Louisiana
Date: c. 1923
Condition: Average; some fading; couple of tears in backing
Quilting: Fan with red thread
Value: $125.00 - $250.00

Comments: Mrs. Jenner spoke only French, but married an Englishman and moved to Louisiana. It seems fitting that a Louisiana quilt should have such a background, does it not?
The edges of the Lily have been embroidered with black thread, a practice not uncommon in appliqued quilts of the 1920's and 1930's.

Photo # 124

Design: Crown of Thorns (New York Beauty, Rocky Mountain Road)
Type: Patchwork
Size: 73″ x 76″
Date: c. 1928
Condition: Excellent
Quilting: Diamonds
Value: $500.00 - $750.00

Photo # 125

Design: Strawberry (Kentucky Beauty)
Type: Patchwork
Size: 63″ x 82″
Maker: Unknown; Kentucky
Date: c. 1930
Condition: Excellent
Quilting: Outline strawberry
Value: $500.00 - $750.00

Comments: Of all the quilts we bought for this book, some far more illustrious and costly, this is one that will not again be on the market. Something about this little quilt touches me. I'll be keeping it. For me, it is truly a Kentucky Beauty!

Photo # 126

Design: Duck Paddle
Type: Patchwork
Size: 74″ x 87″
Maker: Unknown; Kentucky
Date: c. 1928
Condition: Excellent
Quilting: Outline; hearts in green triangle
Value: $500.00 - $750.00

Photo # 123 Courtesy Mr. and Mrs. Earl Hines, Lake Charles, La.

Photo # 124

Photo # 125 Purchased from Anne Bugg, ''Annie's Loft'',
Danville, Ky.

Photo # 126

1925 - 1949

Photo # 127

Design: **Sawtooth**
Type: Patchwork
Size: 78″ x 80″
Maker: Cora Alice Zech, Dark County, Ohio
Date: c. 1928
Condition: Average; edges wavy from use (stretching)
Quilting: Fine lines; tiny stitching
Value: $150.00 - $225.00

Comments: This is a design often seen in Ohio and Indiana quilts. The sawtooth edgings lend drama to a simple, geometric design. The blue coloring seen here is typical of the twenties and thirties.

Photo # 128

Design: **Carpenter's Square** (like Gordian Knot, but not pieced the same)
Type: Patchwork
Size: 82½″ x 84½″
Maker: Unknown; Ohio
Date: c. 1930
Condition: Good
Quilting: Medallions; ¼″ circles; rope border; 9 - 10 stitches per inch; machine edge
Value: $175.00 - $275.00

Photo # 129

Design: **Hands All Around** (differs slightly from Friendship Knot)
Type: Patchwork
Size: 75″ x 82″
Maker: Kate O'Banion Rose
Date: c. 1929
Condition: Excellent
Quilting: Medallions; 8 - 9 stitches per inch
Value: $300.00 - $425.00

Comments: She made all six of her children a quilt in this year. Her stitches are even and tiny. Notice the Four Patch corners.

Photo # 130

Design: **Broken Sugar Bowl**
Type: Patchwork
Size: 69″ x 77″
Maker: Unknown: Indiana
Date: c. 1930
Condition: Average-minus; frayed binding; well used
Quilting: Squares
Value: $150.00 - $250.00

Photo # 127 Courtesy Mr. and Mrs. James Kennon, Ohio.

Photo # 128 Courtesy Leo and Mary K. Walter,
"Stagecoach Antiques", Akron, Ohio

Photo # 129 Courtesy Mr. and Mrs. W. C. Rose,
Owenton, Ky.

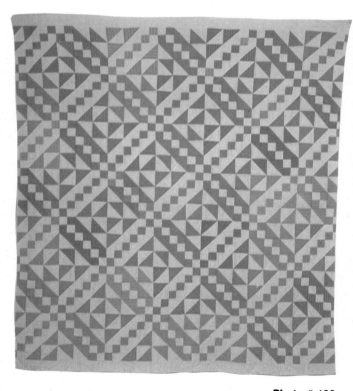

Photo # 130

Photo # 131

Design: **Star of the Bluegrass** (one of a pair)
Type: Patchwork
Size: 71″ x 84″
Maker: Caden Sisters, Lexington, Kentucky
Date: c. 1930
Condition: Excellent
Value: $2,500.00 - $3,000.00 each

Comments: You didn't see too many silk and satin quilts made in the 1930's; and it's extremely rare to find pairs of quilts of any type, let alone pairs of this caliber. There is trapunto work throughout the solid areas and border; the corners are mitered; the stitching is nine per inch. Via the extra tuck-in portion of fabric with selvedge attached, we know the fabric came from Beldings Department Store in Louisville, one of your "better" department stores. (This fabric is a "bonus" for a collection in that it provides an exact match to use should the quilt ever need repairs.)

Photo # 132

Design: **Sampler**
Type: Patchwork
Size: 68″ square
Date: c. 1925
Condition: Good
Quilting: Outline
Value: $800.00 - $1,100.00

Comments: Mrs. Zegart and I believe this quilt was done by a Black artist. It has more stress on color juxtaposition than on line. Do notice the use of colors and the home-drawn shapes of trees, etc. If it could be documented that this was made by an early Black textile artist, more could doubtless be asked for the quilt. Quilts by early Black quilters are becoming more collectible.

In spite of the uneven sashing which is made of random scraps of cloth, this quilt "works."

Photo # 131 Courtesy Mary Virginia Fisher, Lexington, Ky.

Photo # 132 Courtesy Shelly Zegart's Quilts,
Louisville, Ky.

Photo # 133

Design: Whig's Defeat (slight variation)
Type: Patchwork
Size: 76″ x 87½″
Maker: Elizabeth Van Overbeke
Date: c. 1930
Condition: Average
Quilting: Shell and four line; by Women's Quilting Group of Central Christian Church
Value: $450.00 - $600.00

Comments: Mrs. Overbeke copied this from an older quilt in her family that "was of every color in the world, a country quilt made just from the scraps they had."
The pattern dates from the defeat of Lexington's own Henry Clay (Whig Party) for the Presidency in 1844. So, it was a pattern close to Kentuckian's hearts.

Photo # 134

Design: Grapes
Type: Applique (top only)
Size: 80″ x 90″
Maker: Unknown: Northern Ohio
Date: c. 1932
Condition: Average; some staining
Value: $35.00 - $55.00

Comments: Were it not for the staining, this Paragon Company top would be worth $90.00 - $125.00. As it is, unless those rusty leaking-roof stains can be successfully removed, the top is only worthwhile for making pillows. For that, the price must be halved in order to leave a dealer "room" to make a little money after sewing the pillows and buying the stuffing.

Photo # 135

Design: Basket of Tulips
Type: Patchwork Embroidery
Size: 80″ x 82″
Maker: Unknown: Ohio
Date: c. 1932
Condition: Average; some fraying of binding
Quilting: Small squares
Value: $300.00 - $400.00

Comments: Lavender is in vogue now as it was in 1930. This makes quilts in this color easier to sell than ever before. Also, New York is "pushing" the pastel look in quilts; that, too, helps make the 1930's quilts more desirable. It is my understanding that Europe, particularly France, has had a strong market in pastel quilts, particularly lavender, for the past couple of years.

Photo # 136

Design: Colonial Ladies
Type: Applique and Embroidery
Size: 63½″ x 80½″
Maker: Unknown; Kentucky
Date: c. 1930
Condition: Average; one block stained from roof leak
Quilting: Superb; squares and feathered leaves; 14 - 16 stitches per inch
Value: $300.00 - $400.00

Comments: Were it not for the staining in the one block, this quilt would easily be worth two to three times the above. It's really the first quilt I "collected" and has the finest stitching I've ever seen. There are six different ladies, two each. All patches have extensive embroidery work.

Photo # 133 Courtesy Elizabeth Van Overbeke, Lexington, Ky.

Photo # 134

Photo # 135 Courtesy Alice Warobiew, McDonald, Ohio

Photo # 136

Photo # 137

Design: **Morning Glory**
Type: Applique and Embroidery
Size: 68″ x 82″
Maker: Unknown; Lebanon, Tennessee
Date: c. 1928
Condition: Excellent
Quilting: Diamonds, inch apart
Value: $350.00 - $450.00

Comments: The appliques have been buttonhole stitched and stuffed. The batting has cotton seeds; and the binding has been machine stitched. This quilt is quite heavy, having been made not just for decoration but for warmth. It was probably made from a tissue design ordered from a ladies' magazine.

Photo # 138

Design: **Morning Glory**
Type: Applique
Size: 62″ x 84″
Maker: Unknown; Ohio
Date: c. 1930
Condition: Poor; tear at binding
Quilting: Small squares, ½″ apart
Value: $45.00 - $75.00

Comments: My husband accuses me of "adopting" some quilts and this is one of those. Somebody's wonderful quilting was lying there ignored at a market because there's a torn place out of the binding, possibly where it was once caught in those wonderful old coiled spring contraptions that my grandmother fussed were only good for catching dust and snagging covers. It can be salvaged! The binding can be removed, those two inches cut off all around and rebound; or you can use that as your center of emphasis and enlarge the quilt to fit today's beds. Either way, you've saved all those hours quilting, and you've got a bedcover that will serve you for years to come for less than you could buy a new one at the local department store; and it's been hand quilted! It was against my nature to allow it to sit there rejected and destined to become a furniture cover for movers.

Photo # 139

Design: **Broken Star**
Type: Patchwork
Size: 75″ x 76½″
Maker: Blanche Oswalt, Ohio
Date: 1933
Condition: Pink fabric fraying
Quilting: Shell; feather
Value: $100.00 - $150.00

Comments: This quilt was probably a kit. Notice the candy cane border and the Le Moyne Star corner treatments. The pink fabrics need to be repaired.

Photo # 140

Design: **Giant Star Within A Star**
Type: Patchwork
Size: 70″ x 72½″
Maker: Unknown; Ohio
Date: c.1932
Condition: Pink fabric worn
Quilting: Outline; diamond patterned leaves
Value: $100.00 - $150.00

Comments: The pink fabric didn't hold up as well as the blue. Notice the Le Moyne Stars throughout the design. Possibly a kit; but it's past the point of being interesting to a collector.

Photo # 137

Photo # 138

Photo # 139

Photo # 140

Photo # 141

Design: **Unknown**
Type: Applique and Patchwork
Size: 77" x 95"
Maker: Unknown; Indiana
Date: c. 1934
Condition: Good
Quilting: Diagonal lines
Value: $250.00 - $325.00

Photo # 142

Design: **Rose and Irish Chain**
Type: Patchwork
Size: 72" x 84"
Maker: Unknown; Winchester, Kentucky
Date: c. 1933
Condition: Excellent
Quilting: Straight line, 1" apart
Value: $325.00 - $450.00

Comments: Pattern was advertised in *Woman's World* magazine, January, 1933.

Photo # 143

Design: **Fancy Dresden Plate** (family name)
Type: Patchwork and Applique
Size: 76" x 91"
Maker: Ohla Frost, Erie, Pennsylvania
Date: c. 1933
Condition: Poor; worn binding; tiny hole in top edge and backing
Quilting: Exceptional, 12 stitches per inch; outline, leaves and snowflakes
Value: $75.00 - $125.00

Comments: The lady who made this taught sewing for years. The stitching is outstanding. However, the quilt has really been used over the last 50 years and shows it. Its "worth" in today's market lies in the fact that pillows could easily be made from the individual blocks.

Photo # 144

Design: **Dresden Plate** (Friendship Ring; Aster)
Type: Patchwork and Applique
Size: 61½" x 83"
Date: c. 1935
Condition: Poor; binding frayed; spotted; white areas appear missing
Quilting: Diamond and outline
Value: $50.00 - $75.00

Comments: A dealer brought this to me and I told him I didn't want it. Why? Dresden Plate is a very common pattern for quilts and collectors ignore them. The reason I didn't want THIS one, however, is because the plates were pieced with white and very pastel fabrics. It makes the design look as if parts of it are missing. I wound up buying it simply to picture it and show you what NOT to buy. It was probably a good move. I have since seen at least ten Dresden Plate quilts with this same problem; but the prices asked certainly haven't reflected that condition! In our shop, the people who "like" Dresden Plate designs are the people who "remember" Mother or Grandmother having one and who want one for that reason. They WILL sell, but not at phenomenal prices.

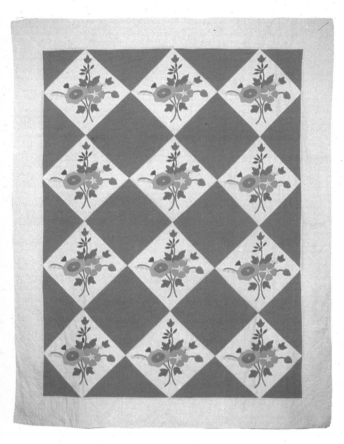

Photo # 142

Photo # 141 Courtesy Rick Norton, Noblesville, Ind.

Photo # 143

Photo # 144

91

Photo # 145

Design: Sawtooth
Type: Patchwork
Size: 74¼" x 75"
Maker: Unknown; Illinois
Date: c. 1933
Condition: Excellent
Quilting: Diamonds, feathered leaves, medallions; 9 stitches per inch
Value: $500.00 - $750.00

Photo # 146

Design: Embroidered Flowers
Type: Embroidery and Patchwork
Size: 75½" x 77"
Maker: Unknown; Ohio
Date: c. 1933
Condition: Excellent
Quilting: Diamonds, circles, straight line; 9 stitches per inch
Value: $325.00 - $400.00

Photo # 147

Design: Goblet
Type: Patchwork
Size: 72" x 82"
Date: c. 1932
Condition: Good
Quilting: Triple line
Value: $225.00 - $300.00

Comments: It's rather unusual to find a quilt made in this pattern even though it was featured in several newspapers of the early 1930's; and ''everyone'' copied the newspaper designs! It was also made in reds and white, a combination that appeals to many of today's collectors.

Photo # 148

Design: Wind Blown Tulips
Type: Applique
Size: 92" x 97"
Maker: Attributed to Geisler family, Ferdinand, Indiana
Date: c. 1935
Condition: Excellent
Quilting: Diamond and unlinked diamond chains
Value: $900.00 - $1,200.00

Comments: Tulips have ever been popular designs with the German ''Dutch'' people from which this quilt springs. Wind Blown Tulips was a popular design with everyone in the 1930's; but notice the extra tulips ''growing'' around the border of this quilt, doubtless a contribution of this quilter to the basic design.
   ''Ice Cream (Cone)'' borders were a commonly used border treatment during the 1930's.

Photo # 145

Photo # 146

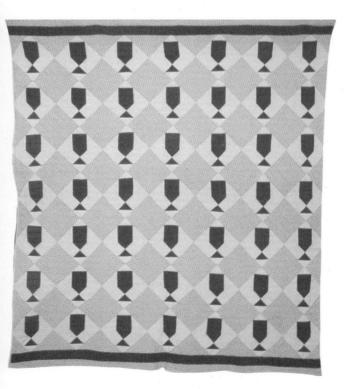

Photo # 148 Courtesy Ruth Margarida, Jasper, Ind.

Photo # 147 Courtesy Rick Norton,
"Hornet's Nest Antiques", Noblesville, Ind.

1925 - 1949

Photo # 149

Design: **Lone Star**
Type: Patchwork
Size: 71″ x 72″
Maker: Mrs. Robert (Sarah) Lucas, Owen County, Kentucky
Date: c. 1935
Condition: Excellent
Quilting: Shell at corners; outline elsewhere
Value: $350.00 - $500.00

Comments: Notice the "twisted ribbon" effect given the border.
The story goes that her son, Paul, came in and saw her working on this and exclaimed, "That's the prettiest quilt I ever saw!" When she became ill in the 1940's, she told the family that this quilt was to be Paul's since he "liked it"! She wanted her work left where it would be appreciated.

Photo # 150

Design: **Postage Stamp Trip Around The World**
Type: Patchwork
Size: 71″ x 77″
Maker: Unknown; Indianapolis, Indiana
Date: c. 1934
Condition: Average
Quilting: Outline
Value: $75.00 - $125.00

Comments: The "postage stamp" quilts came into vogue toward the end of the miniaturization craze. They "died out" around the mid-1940's; although I did see a lovely one hanging in the Bell Buckle, Tennessee, NQA show in 1983, so they haven't totally expired.

Photo # 151

Design: **Yo Yo**
Type: Pieced
Size: 70″ x 75″ excluding the pillow sham
Date: c. 1934
Condition: Excellent
Quilting: Not applicable
Value: $150.00 - $200.00

Comments: Piecing "yo yo" pillow slips and quilts was a rage of the late 1920's and 1930's. Yo yos are made of circles that are gathered around the edges; the edges are drawn together; the resulting "bag" is flattened with the hole at the center section. Then, when enough of these are made, they're whipped together on four sides forming the lattice like covering. They're always very colorful; they're NOT always pretty. This one has the added dimension of a design and it's exceptionally pretty.
I overheard a lady at a market exclaiming at the bargain she'd found in a Yo Yo spread. "It was only $125.00!" she was telling her friend. It wasn't nearly as attractive as this! I've seen prices from $75.00 to $380.00. People seem either to love them or hate them.
This spread has 2,268 yo yo pieces. It took quite some time to make.

Photo # 152

Design: **Birds**
Type: Patchwork and Embroidery
Size: 81″ square
Maker: Mrs. Eckert, Dubois County, Indiana
Date: c. 1935
Condition: Excellent
Quilting: Squares and cable border
Value: $750.00 - $1,000.00

Comments: This is the finest embroidery work on a quilt that I've seen! The birds are entirely covered with a cable or chain stitch such as seen in museum pieces!

Photo # 149 Courtesy Marie Spicer Lucas, Lexington, Ky.

Photo # 150

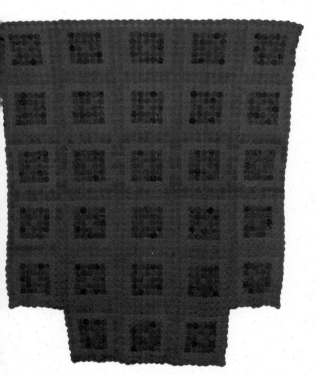

Photo # 151 Courtesy Irene Gilcrist, Doylestown, Ohio

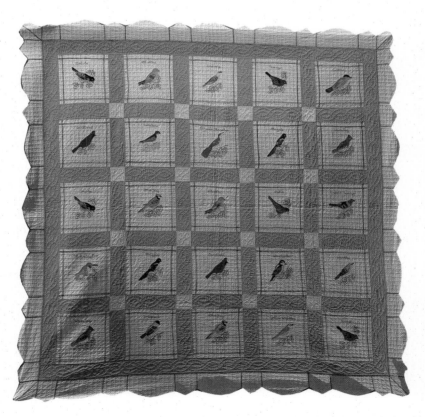

Photo # 152 Courtesy Ruth Margarida, Jasper, Ind.

1925 - 1949

Photo # 153

Design: Tulips
Type: Applique
Size: 82" x 83¼"
Maker: Maude Lowry Hood, Cambridge, Ohio
Date: 1930
Condition: Excellent
Quilting: Diamonds 5/8", feathered medallions; 9 stitches per inch
Value: $450.00 - $750.00

Comments: This obviously is a kit design as swag borders with looped corners are especially noted kit treatments. Generally, collectors will not pay beyond $1,500.00 for a quilt they know to be a kit design, no matter how well executed since the kit factor doubtless means there are others "like" it. However, it may be a misguided attitude when a particularly fine example is encountered. A great quilt is just that. You could give the same kit to a hundred quilters and you'd get probably 20 good ones; five really excellent ones and one superb one! I don't think collectors should be ignoring those last six; but particularly not that one outstanding example of skill. This quilt is flawed only by the misalignment of tulip colors.

Photo # 154

Design: Tulips
Type: Applique
Date: c. 1930
Condition: Excellent
Quilting: None - top only
Value: Asking price, $295.00

Comments: Closely resembling the preceding quilt, this was probably another company's pattern as the petals of the tulips and the border treatment are different.

Quilt top prices range from as little as $5.00 at a local yard sale to as high as $2,800.00 at an antique show (for an 1860's album type). Generally, they sell from $50.00 to $150.00, depending on the fabrics and the design. Rates to quilt a top vary but generally range from $150.00 to $225.00; however, the lowest I've heard of was $65.00 in Michigan; the highest, $250.00 in Ohio.

Photo # 155

Design: Butterfly
Type: Patchwork
Maker: Emma Jane Koeninger (1902-1974), Newlin, Texas
Date: 1936
Condition: Good
Quilting: Outline
Value: $275.00 - $350.00

Comments: This is only one of many "Butterfly" patterns that have been popular with quilters since the 1930's. Not all these types are "butterflies", however; I ran into one 1930's "moth" pattern and one "dragon fly" as I did my research.

Many of the fabrics in this quilt are from feed sacks. That used to be a detriment but I suspect that the time will soon come when that's a big "plus.". Many farm ladies washed, ironed and used the materials from the sacks of chicken feed to make children's clothing and quilts.

Photo # 156

Design: Double Wedding Ring
Type: Patchwork
Maker: Emma Jane Koeninger, Newlin, Texas
Date: 1937
Condition: Good
Quilting: Outline and medallion
Value: $275.00 - $375.00

Comments: Again, most of the fabrics here are from feed sacks.
If "everyone" has a Flower Garden quilt in their family first, and a Dresden Plate second, then the third most common design is a Double Wedding Ring. Of the three, love for this pattern has lingered longest. Collectors, however, view anything commonly found with varying degrees of disdain. Collectors are willing to pay more to get what they want. The general public is hard pressed to part with $300.00 for a quilt--which is about what it costs to make one today.

Photo # 153

Photo # 154 Courtesy Mr. and Mrs. Allen Showwalter,
Doylestown, Ohio

Photo # 155 Courtesy Mr. and Mrs. Dowden
Koeninger, Sundown, Texas

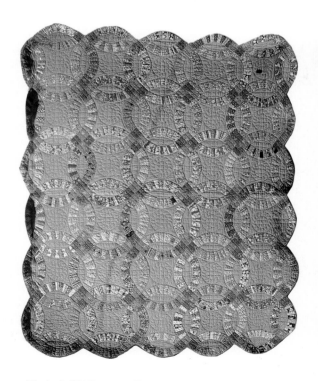

Photo # 156 Courtesy Dowden and Bonnie Koeninger,
Sundown, Texas

Photo # 157

Design: Apple Blossom
Type: Applique
Size: 68″ x 83″
Maker: Fannie Rose, Owen County, Kentucky
Date: c. 1930
Condition: Average; some fading
Quilting: Diamonds (1 inch)
Value: $150.00 - $200.00

Comments: This is Sterns & Foster "Mountain Mist" pattern #80.

Photo # 158

Design: Deco Flowers (original)
Type: Applique and Patchwork
Maker: Dora Frederking, Okawville, Illinois
Date: c. 1930
Condition: Excellent
Value: $650.00 - $800.00

Photo # 159

Design: Unknown
Type: Applique
Size: 79½″ square
Date: c. 1936
Condition: Excellent
Quilting: Diamonds (1¼″), medallions, feathers; 7 stitches per inch
Value: $500.00 - $750.00

Comments: This is undoubtedly a kit quilt whose design and sometimes fabric make-up have been supplied by a manufacturer. Quilting from kits was extremely popular from the early 1930's onward. You can still see the pencil marks where the quilter marked the design. By the way, pencil marks are hard to remove from fabric. Today it is not recommended as a way of marking fabrics; but it was a universally used way of marking patterns in earlier quilts. VERY early quilters used powdered "bluing" and colored chalk powder which was bagged and "daubed" onto the stencil holes. I've also heard of straight line quilting being marked by husbands with their carpenter's chalk lines (where a chalked line is drawn across the top of the quilt and snapped to leave a line of chalk behind to use as a pattern.) Soap slivers were also used to mark quilts. All these type markings, of course, would wash out with the first laundering. That is NOT the case with pencil markings.

Photo # 160

Design: Rose Tree
Type: Applique
Size: 72″ x 91″
Maker: Unknown; Kentucky
Date: c. 1938
Condition: Excellent
Quilting: Outline; diamonds; done in pink thread, 8 stitches per inch
Value: $750.00 - $1,000.00

Comments: This is a Sterns & Foster "Mountain Mist" pattern that was advertised in their 1938 catalogue. I was told by the dealer from whom I bought it that the owner firmly remembered it as having been made in 1912! Thus, owner memory is not always accurate. The quilt is unwashed and marvelously executed. One of the petals of each rose design has been stuffed.

Photo # 157 Courtesy Mr. and Mrs. Arvin Rose, Owenton, Ky.

Photo # 158 Courtesy Spirit of America, St. Louis, Mo.

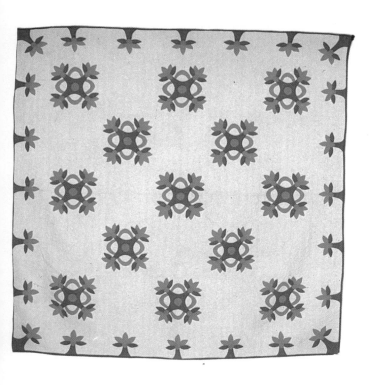

Photo # 159

Photo # 160

Photo # 161

Design: **Chalice and Birds** (original)
Type: Applique
Size: 78″ x 87″
Maker: Women in Parrish for Father Bazell
Date: c. 1925
Condition: Excellent
Quilting: Squares, diamonds, feathering, etc.
Value: $1,500.00 - $2,000.00

Comments: This is the type quilt that can only get better.

Photo # 162

Design: **Tulips**
Type: Applique
Size: 65″ x 78″
Maker: Unknown; Lebanon, Tennessee
Date: c. 1936
Condition: Average; some bleeding of materials from washing
Quilting: Diamond (1 inch); 8 stitches per inch
Value: $150.00 - $225.00

Comments: Some of the appliques are done by hand; some machine stitched! The backing and ground material are both muslin. The half design is different green fabric from the rest. Pencil markings are still visible. This design probably came via newspaper or magazine; but the fabrics chosen give this a "folk" appearance that I find very endearing.

Photo # 163

Design: **Pictorial**
Type: Patchwork and Applique
Date: c. 1936
Condition: Excellent
Quilting: Outline; feathered leaves, medallions, fish
Value: $5,000.00 - $6,000.00

Comments: You seldom find pictorial work in older quilts, but it's always treasured by collectors when it is discovered. This is a particular jewel with the quaint charm of a Grandma Moses-type painting with scenes from a way of life long past. The animals and people are worked with particular skill. (Representations of people in quilts are rarely seen!) Further, these are not stick figures, but pictured in motion!

Notice the rooster weathervane on the steeple; the children and dog beneath the tree; the shadow below the grazing cow; the Appaloosa or dappled horse and rider; the deacon with the umbrella; the filled-to-capacity buggy; the rick-rack picket fence around the church; the clock and gothic windows of the church itself; and the use of fabric to portray the surrounding fields, mountains and orchards.

The only thing hurting this quilt is the loss of the name of the person who did it. I've seen pictorial quilts with less going for them (but complete with "history") valued as high as $20,000.00. (I haven't seen them SELL for that, but I've seen them valued that high in private collections.)

Photo # 164

Design: **Dancing Daffodils**
Type: Applique
Size: 65″ x 81″
Maker: Marie Spicer Lucas, Owen County, Kentucky
Date: 1938
Condition: Average-minus; some fading and worn fabric
Quilting: Diamonds (¾″) and spider web motif in center of flowers
Value: $125.00 - $175.00

Comments: This is Sterns & Foster "Mountain Mist" design #24 which was advertised in their 1938 catalogue. I recently saw this design in better condition at an antique shop in central Kentucky for $345.00. My mother remembers this from her girlhood as "the prettiest quilt I'd ever seen!"

Photo # 161 Courtesy Ruth Margarida, Jasper, Ind.

Photo # 162

Photo # 163 Courtesy James Brooks, American Antiques,
W. Redding, Ct.

Photo # 164 Courtesy Mrs. Pauline Lucas, Washington, D.C.

Photo # 165

Design: Sunbonnet Sue
Type: Patchwork and Applique
Maker: Mary Cauble
Date: 1938
Condition: Good
Quilting: Diamond and medallions
Value: $175.00 - $225.00

Comments: The border and appliques of this quilt have been machine stitched using the same color thread as the fabric.

Photo # 166

Design: Lone Star
Type: Patchwork
Maker: Mary Cauble (b. 1889)
Date: 1937
Condition: Excellent
Quilting: Diamonds
Value: $350.00 - $500.00

Comments: This quilt was made for her nephew, Robert, on the occasion of his graduation from high school. This, then, was his "freedom" quilt, an old time tradition where members of a boy's family would gather and make him a quilt on his graduation or coming of age. It was the boy's equivalent of an engagement quilt made for a girl by her friends.

Photo # 167

Design: Wild Duck
Type: Applique
Size: 82" square
Maker: Unknown; Dubois County, Indiana
Date: 1938
Condition: Excellent
Quilting: Feathered chains and medallions; flowers
Value: $1,100.00 - $1,500.00

Comments: This is Sterns & Foster's "Mountain Mist" pattern #45 as advertised in their 1938 catalogue. It's a striking design and has been handled here by an expert quilter.

Photo # 168

Design: Sawtooth
Type: Patchwork
Size: 78" x 80"
Maker: Unknown; Dubois County, Indiana
Date: c. 1939
Condition: Excellent
Quilting: Diamonds; tulips; waving line border
Value: $800.00 - $1,000.00

Comments: This quilt has the two "right" colors -- blue and white -- and fantastic quilting. What more could you want?

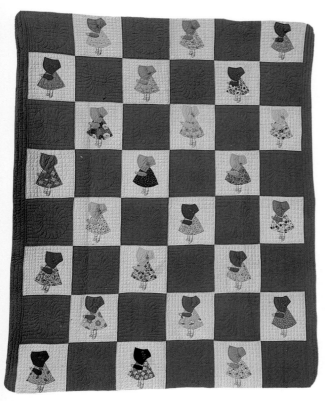

Photo # 165 Courtesy Harry and Anita Wood, Odessa, Texas

Photo # 166 Courtesy Harry and Anita Wood, Odessa, Texas

Photo # 167 Courtesy Ruth Margarida, Jasper, Ind.

Photo # 168 Courtesy Ruth Margarida, Jasper, Ind.

1925 - 1949

Photo # 169

Design: **Orange Blossom**
Type: Applique
Maker: Unknown; Dubois County, Indiana
Date: c. 1939
Condition: Excellent
Quilting: Diagonal line; feather medallions; outline; 11 to 12 stitches per inch
Value: $1,250.00 - $1,500.00

Comments: This is Sterns & Foster "Mountain Mist" pattern #53 which was advertised in their 1938 catalogue. This particular quilt was a wedding gift which was never used. It has lovely quilting!

Photo # 170

Design: **Small Triangle Variation** (the maker left the center patches as a whole square rather than cutting them into triangles)
Type: Patchwork (Double Quilt)
Size: 66″ x 86″
Maker: Louise Patterson, Millersburg, Kentucky
Date: c. 1940
Condition: Excellent
Quilting: Outline and medallions (in squares)
Value: $175.00 - $250.00

Comments: This quilt is EXACTLY THE SAME on the REVERSE side! It's the most unusual quilt in its manner of construction that I've seen. Each PIECE is a small quilt or "potholder" type piece. All the separate pieces have been whip-stitched together as one does the Yo Yo or Cathedral Window quilts.

If the designer had bothered to carry out the "cubed" effect seen in a couple of the squares, this quilt would be worth twice as much!

Photo # 171

Design: **Crown of Thorns** (New York Beauty, Rocky Mountain Road, Crossroads to Jerusalem)
Type: Patchwork
Size: 75″ x 76″
Date: c. 1938
Quilting: Half and quarter moon quilting; 8 stitches per inch
Value: $650.00 - $900.00

Photo # 172

Design: **Fannie's Fan**
Type: Patchwork
Size: 70½″ x 88″
Maker: Carrie Lloyd and Mildred Mitman
Date: 1938
Condition: Average-minus; some fading; some fabric wear
Quilting: Diamonds (1 inch) and outline
Value: $125.00 - $175.00

Comments: Fan designs in quilts have been popular since the 1880's. This quilt is said to still elicit compliments every time it is put on the bed for company.

Photo # 169 Courtesy Ruth Margarida, Jasper, Ind.

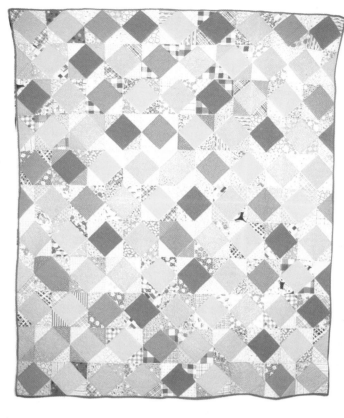

Photo # 170 Courtesy Mr. and Mrs. Maurice Rice,
Lexington, Ky.

Photo # 171 Courtesy Peggy Tobias, Uniontown, Ohio

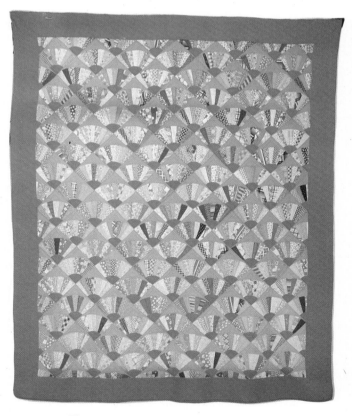

Photo # 172 Courtesy Mr. and Mrs. Ernest Mitman,
Washington Court House, Ohio

1925 - 1949

Photo # 173

Design: **Zodiac**
Type: Patchwork, Applique and Embroidery
Size: 88″ x 108″
Maker: Edith F. Cross (1867 - 1968); Oakland, Maryland
Date: c. 1940
Condition: Good; some fading
Quilting: Quarter moons
Value: $350.00 - $500.00

Comments: This quilt was made from a pattern taken from the Akron *Beacon Journal*. This fits with the interest in the stars, reading tea leaves and playing Ouija™ board games that prevailed in that time period. The size of the quilt is unusual for a 1940's bed.

Photo # 174

Design: **Strip**
Type: Patchwork Stripes
Size: 61″ x 77″
Maker: Unknown; Eastern Kentucky
Date: c. 1944
Condition: Used; torn; some fabrics loose and need restitching
Quilting: Straight line, 1½″ alternating with ½″
Value: $75.00 - $125.00

Comments: This was a popular way of using scraps of material. You could sew various strips together, cut them into blocks and then stitch the blocks together.

In this thickly padded quilt, the quilter has created design by the manner in which she put the strips together; that may not have been an original idea since the technique was shown in a 1944 newspaper.

Modern quilters of no little repute, Nancy Crow and Michael James, to name just two, are using this basic technique of strip quilting to create masterpieces of color and design. Their works are meticulously constructed, however, with a view to contrasting or complimentary color schemes and interweaving and intersecting lines. They've taken the technique into another dimension, so to speak. I probably shouldn't speak of their work here on the same page with this mountain quilter's. On the other hand, this quilter has achieved an orderly sort of beauty from the chaos of her particular supply of fabrics. You have to respect the creation of beauty from practically nothing.

Photo # 175

Design: **Little Boy's Breeches**
Type: Patchwork
Size: 67″ x 83″
Maker: Eva Owens, Western Kentucky
Date: c. 1943
Condition: Good
Quilting: Outline
Value: $125.00 - $200.00

Comments: Maybe it takes a country girl to appreciate this quilt, but I had no sooner walked by it than it hit me that it's a Kentucky type quilt! I was thinking Eastern Kentucky mountains; it turned out that the lady's husband was a miner in Western Kentucky when she made this. I can remember my great aunt, Alice, giggling over this pattern and showing my child's eyes where to see the breeches in the design.

You will find some quilts lined with blankets. That's not at all unusual in Kentucky. You used what you had on hand; and I've heard many say that blankets are easier to quilt on; warmer and less heavy to sleep under; and easier to wash because they didn't bunch up like cotton batting did.

Photo # 173 Courtesy Peggy Tobias, Uniontown, Ohio

Photo # 174

Photo # 175 Purchased from Paulette Schwartz,
"Magnolia's Old Red Barn", Centralia, Ill.

Photo # 176

Design: **Job's Troubles** (Four Point Star, Kite, Snowball, Periwinkle, Danish Stars [1942] and Crazy Star)
Type: Patchwork
Size: 69″ x 81″
Maker: Belle Cox
Date: c. 1940
Condition: Good
Quilting: Outline
Value: $125.00 - $200.00

Photo # 177

Design: **Seven Sisters** (Seven Stars)
Type: Patchwork
Size: 76″ x 80″
Maker: Myra Cooper Ayers
Date: c. 1940
Condition: Excellent
Quilting: Machine
Value: $125.00 - $200.00

Photo # 178

Design: **Snowflake**
Type: Applique
Size: 90″ x 78″
Date: c. 1942
Condition: Good; some border fraying
Quilting: Outline and feathered motifs; 9 stitches per inch
Value: $750.00 - $1,000.00

Comments: We bought this at the annual Genesee Valley Center Quilt Show in Flint, Michigan, where it won third place as Viewer's Choice. The owner later wrote me to give me that information and to say that she was glad that many people would get to see it in the book rather than having it stuck away in storage. The original owners moved to California.

As we had it on the wall to photograph, a dealer interested in quilts came by and said she'd received one exactly like it in green for her wedding in 1942. She also said she'd just seen one hanging in a shop in New York for $1,200.00! It's definitely a kit; "Snowflower" was the title used at the show.

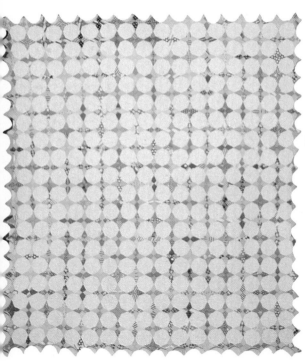

Photo # 176 Courtesy Becky Alexander, Uniontown, Ohio

Photo # 177 Courtesy Mr. and Mrs. Atwood Ayers, Owenton, Ky.

Photo # 178

1925 - 1949

Photo # 179

Design: **Four Patch**
Type: Patchwork and Embroidered; Friendship
Size: 84″ square
Makers: Various: Minnie Butts, Mae Beard, Kathryn Sharp, to name a few
Date: c. 1943
Condition: Good
Quilting: Straight line;
Value: $175.00 - $250.00

Comments: Strictly speaking, this is a Patriotic quilt. It was made by these ladies to honor their sons while they were away fighting in the war, hence, the color scheme.

Other names appearing on the quilt include the following: Lydia Sheets, Edna Epperson, Deane Osborne, Hazel Guy and Nellie McKinney.

Photo # 180

Design: **Stars 'n Stripes**
Type: Patchwork
Date: c. 1943
Condition: Good; needs some patches resewn
Quilting: Top only
Value: $125.00 - $200.00

Comments: This top has some thirties fabrics in it; but the red and white striped stars make me think it's forties war patriotism here rather than the '26 sesquicentennial patriotism. I could be wrong. Whatever, it was nicely done. There are 64 stars. (Sometimes you can figure dates by counting the number of stars in the flags or the number of states mentioned in the embroidered types. There should be fifty after 1959!)

This is the type of top that's certainly worth salvaging. Quilting it now will never make it worth what the quilt would have been had it been quilted in its own time frame; but it would have worth above and beyond normal tops. Lest you think you could fool someone into thinking it was quilted in the thirties or forties, I should tell you that thread made since about 1963 "glows" under a black light. That's a test some collectors will subject a quilt to in order to determine if it has been repaired or not. Repairs should ALWAYS be noted. To some collectors, it will not make a difference; to others, repairs mean "No sale!" It's frequently better to leave a quilt "as is" than to tamper with it.

Photo # 181

Design: **Nine Patch and Le Moyne Stars** (similar to Cluster of Stars)
Type: Patchwork and Applique
Size: 69½″ x 85″
Maker: Effie Lawrence and Daisy Johnson
Date: c. 1950
Condition: Excellent
Quilting: Outline
Value: $150.00 - $250.00

Photo # 182

Design: **Dahlia** (Star Flower, Golden Glow, Missouri Daisy)
Type: Patchwork and Applique
Size: 78″ x 88″
Maker: Unknown; Winchester, Kentucky
Date: c. 1950
Condition: Excellent
Quilting: Outline; medallions; stars and chained diamond border
Value: $125.00 - $200.00

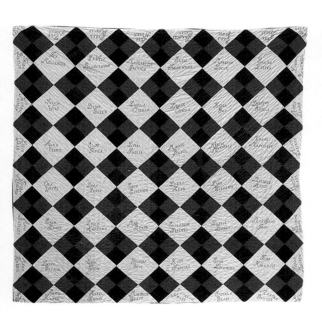

Photo # 179 Courtesy Rick Norton, Noblesville, Ind.

Photo # 180 Courtesy Mrs. Frank Lovell, Versailles, Ky.

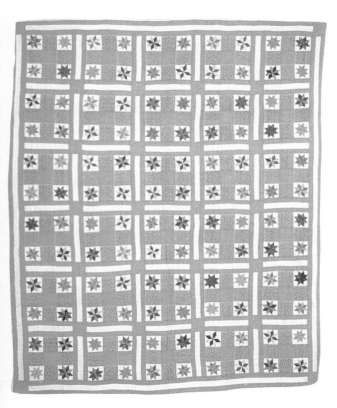

Photo # 181 Courtesy Mr. and Mrs. Atwood Ayers,
Owenton, Ky.

Photo # 182 Purchased from Sandy Roundtree,
Winchester, Ky.

Photo # 183

Design: **Blossom** (original)
Type: Patchwork, Applique and Embroidery
Size: 68″ x 82″
Maker: Rosemary Cox
Date: 1954
Condition: Good; some fraying of edges
Quilting: Outline and medallion
Value: $150.00 - $275.00

Photo # 184

Design: **Sunflower**
Type: Applique
Size: 69″ x 89″
Maker: Unknown; Pennsylvania
Date: c. 1950
Condition: Excellent
Quilting: Diamonds, leaves and medallions; 5 stitches per inch
Value: $225.00 - $350.00

Comments: This is Sterns & Foster "Mountain Mist" pattern #P as advertised in their 1938 catalogue. However, due to the dark green colored fabric used in the quilt, I believe it was made later than that. I also believe this to have been someone's first effort at making a quilt and possibly was made by a child. The patches are crudely cut and the stitching is very large and uneven. In spite of all this, the very primtive sewing manages to lend the quilt a kind of charm. It makes you smile to look at it!

Photo # 185

Design: **Friendship Plume**
Type: Applique
Size: 79″ x 93″
Maker: Mrs. Rohleder, Dubois County, Indiana
Date: c. 1950
Condition: Good
Quilting: Outline and Log Cabin squares; 9 - 10 stitches per inch
Value: $250.00 - $350.00

Comments: This is Sterns & Foster "Mountain Mist" pattern #59 as advertised in their 1938 catalogue. This was as close as I could come to a Hawaiian-type quilt where the entire quilt covering design is cut as a single piece from fabric and appliqued to the quilt top. Here, they've done the same basic technique, but they've cut it into six manageable patches that are subsequently sewn together.

Photo # 186

Design: **Rising Star** (Novel Star, Hexagonal Star, Morning Star, Tennessee Star)
Type: Patchwork
Size: 87½″ x 96″
Maker: Cathy Gaines Florence, Lexington, Kentucky
Date: 1956
Condition: Excellent
Quilting: Outline
Value: $150.00 - $275.00

Comments: I include this for two reasons: one, to show I had actually made a quilt and two, to point out that it's necessary to look for the "youngest" fabric in a quilt. Many of the stars are made of scraps from my own 1950's dresses; but many are made from fabrics I got from the camel-backed trunk residing in the upstairs hallway of my grandmother's home. It had nothing in it but scraps of fabrics. I remember I had picked several rayon and silk fabrics but my grandmother said those were hard to sew on and I'd have to back those with paper in order to make the points of the stars come out right. So, I put those back and chose cottons. The pattern came from thumbing through an old *Progressive Farmer* magazine and spotting a small "pattern of the month" or some such feature. I drew and cut the pattern (only three tries to get the diamonds to meet properly) and happily occupied myself for the next few weeks of summer "sewing my quilt stars."

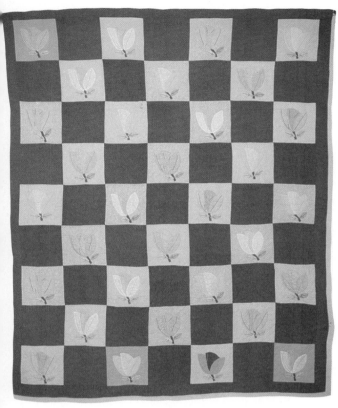

Photo # 183 Courtesy Rosemary Cox, Uniontown, Ohio

Photo # 184 Purchased from Todd's Square Antique Mall, Lexington, Ky.

Photo # 185

Photo # 186

Photo # 187

Design: Cathedral Window
Type: Patchwork
Size: 63″ x 73″
Maker: Louise Jacoby Wilmont
Date: c. 1955
Condition: Excellent
Value: $225.00 - $325.00

Comments: In the manner in which this is constructed, the "quilting" is done as each patch is made. I've heard several quilters who have made these say that they'd "never make another one." It's a long procedure. Their marketable value, at present, in no way reflects the effort put into making one.

Photo # 188

Design: Cathedral Window
Type: Patchwork
Size: 56″ x 74″
Maker: Fannie Rose, Owen County, Kentucky
Date: c. 1969
Condition: Excellent
Value: $225.00 - $325.00

Comments: This has been put together in the traditional way of making two patches exactly alike and setting them opposite each other. The dating between the two quilts shown here encompasses the time period when making these type quilts was at its peak. The idea of the quilt was to make it look like stained glass windows and it takes a skillful use of colors to get a pleasing whole quilt. It's hard to hold a "whole" image in one's mind when making tiny, single squares. Therefore, should you attempt one of these, it would be a good idea to put the COLORS on graph paper FIRST. That way you know the effect of the whole quilt. Some people "solve" this dilemma by making the quilt of only one color (see above); but that really defeats the purpose of the pattern.

Photo # 189

Design: Rising Star (Hexagonal Star, Novel Star, Morning Star, Tennessee Star)
Type: Patchwork
Size: 69″ x 82″
Maker: Lou Anne Ingram, Madison County, Kentucky
Date: c. 1958
Condition: Excellent
Quilting: Outline; 9 stitches per inch
Value: $225.00 - $325.00

Photo # 190

Design: Rosary (original)
Type: Applique
Size: 79″ x 90″
Maker: Women of Parish, Ferdinand, Indiana
Date: c. 1950
Condition: Excellent
Quilting: Straight line and fleurettes
Value: $1,200.00 - $1,500.00

Comments: This quilt was made by some women in the parish to be raffled at a church bazaar. It was a way of raising money, a practice often done, even today. These types of quilts (made for special functions and purposes) are probably very good investments. This one certainly should be as it's an original design, of a religious theme (not often encountered), has the "right" colors and is beautifully quilted!

Photo # 187 Courtesy Louise Jacoby Wilmont,
Green Acres, Georgetown, Ky.

Photo # 188 Courtesy Mr. and Mrs. Arvin Rose,
Owenton, Ky.

Photo # 189 Courtesy of Mrs. Helen Dennis,
Lexington, Ky.

Photo # 190 Courtesy Ruth Margarida, Jasper, Ind.

Photo # 191

Design: Tulips
Type: Applique and Patchwork
Size: 77" x 102"
Maker: Unknown; Indiana
Date: c. 1960
Condition: Good
Quilting: Diamonds, 1¾"
Value: $150.00 - $200.00

Photo # 192

Design: Rising Sun Variation
Type: Patchwork and Applique
Size: 64" x 84"
Maker: Mrs. Riggins
Date: c. 1962
Condition: Excellent
Quilting: Fleurettes and outline
Value: $350.00 - $425.00

Photo # 193

Design: The Four X Quilt
Type: Patchwork
Size: 67" x 79"
Maker: Elsie Mae Gaines, Owen County, Kentucky
Date: 1965
Condition: Excellent
Quilting: Outline
Value: $125.00 - $200.00

Comments: This is our marriage quilt, a gift from my grandmother. I wonder what four crossroads of life she had in mind. The four that come to my mind are birth, marriage, children, and death.

Photo # 194

Design: Maple Leaf (sans stem)
Type: Patchwork
Size: 93" x 98"
Date: June, 1971
Condition: Good; small stain on front
Quilting: Diamonds; leaves, medallions
Value: $145.00 - $185.00

Comments: This quilt would be more valuable had the person put the stem on the leaf. However, this could still be added via embroidery to improve the appearance of the quilt.

Photo # 191

Photo # 192

Photo # 193 Courtesy Mr. and Mrs. Gene Florence, Jr.,
Lexington, Ky.

Photo # 194 Courtesy of Alice Warobiew,
Brookfield, Ohio

Photo # 195

Design: **Turkey Tracks Variation** (Wandering Foot)
Type: Patchwork
Size: 72″ x 98″
Maker: Lou Anne Ingram, Madison County, Kentucky
Date: c. 1964
Condition: Excellent
Quilting: Straight line and medallion; 9 stitches per inch
Value: $600.00 - $850.00

Comments: The addition of a tiny square block at the corner of the basic Turkey Track patch lends to this the look of an Irish Chain which adds a new dimension to the design, allowing it to be doubly traditional and new and "modern" at the same time. Her choice of design and color has made this quilt very graphic, something a collector is always seeking in a quilt. Notice, too, the added drama created by the bold border and corner treatment. She made at least two quilts from this design. The other is a lovely gold and white which she gave to her granddaugther on the occasion of her marriage.

Dealers have told me time and again that TWO COLOR quilts sell better than do multicolored ones and the best combinations of colors are blue and white and red and white.

Photo # 196

Design: Copied from a woven coverlet (probably a Chariot Wheel design)
Type: Patchwork
Size: 90″ x 114″
Date: 1973
Condition: Excellent
Quilting: Diamond
Value: $500.00 - $750.00

Comments: The interesting thing about this quilt is that this was inspired by the owner having seen the design on a woven coverlet at a flea market. He went home and at his design desk, adapted the design for a quilt, picked out the fabric he wanted and gave it to some ladies he knows who did the actual quilt making. Totally unknown to him was the fact that Sterns & Foster has a "Mountain Mist" pattern of this exact pattern -- #34, called Homespun -- and it is advertised being done in a red and white color scheme! Do notice the border treatment, however, as laid out by Dr. Levy. That is unusual!

Photo # 195 Courtesy Mrs. Hazel Dennis,
Lexington, Ky.

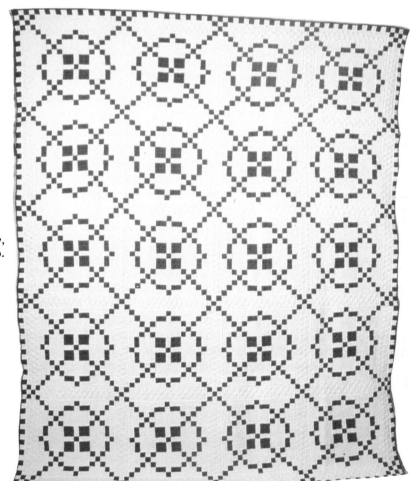

Photo # 196 Courtesy of Dr. Jerome Levy,
Creve Coeur, Mo.

Photo # 197

Design: **Fishing Freddie**
Type: Patchwork and Fabric Paint
Size: 71½" x 87½"
Maker: Sibyl Gaines and Marie Lucas, Fayette County, Kentucky
Date: 1975
Condition: Excellent
Quilting: Straight line; fleurettes
Value: $125.00 - $175.00

Comments: The flowers and fishing line on this quilt have been hand drawn using fabric paints. This mode of "embroidery" is being increasingly used and I felt it ought to be represented here.

Photo # 198

Design: **Holly Hobby**™
Type: Applique and Embroidery
Size: 39" x 59"
Maker: Unknown; Salt Lake City, Utah
Date: c. 1978
Condition: Excellent
Quilting: Tied
Value: $125.00 - $200.00

Comments: Ostensibly, this was made as a little girl's crib quilt. However, the padding and ruffling are so thick and wide that it could be used as little more than a decoration for the bed rather than having a child sleep under it.

The girl figure has lace bloomers and a petticoat under her apron protected dress. It's a delightful little quilt and very representative of its time. Holly Hobby™ is the present day equivalent of the 1920's beloved Sunbonnet.

Photo # 199, 200, 201

Design: **Peacock Revolution in Kentucky** (Variation of Grandma's Peacock)
Type: Patchwork
Size: 68¼" x 85"
Maker: Peggy Clem
Date: 1971-1972
Condition: Excellent
Quilting: Outline
Value: $1,500.00 - $1,750.00

Comments: Mrs. Clem disliked the design of the Peacock's body in the original pattern, found one in a children's story book that she liked better, had it enlarged four times and HER peacock was born. Further, she decided to give all peacocks a "personality" and after including family, she sewed notable Kentuckians of that time frame into her quilt. You see Adolph Rupp, retiring and gripping a basketball; Colonel Harland Sanders of Kentucky Fried Chicken fame with his memorable white hat, cane and mustache; John Y. Brown, Jr. running on the Democratic Party ticket with bright ideas; Gay Brewer with his golf club; Don Brumfield, jockey, winning the 98th Kentucky Derby; Whitney Young, the Black equal rights leader who died in 1971, balancing the black and white issues; then Kentucky Governor Wendell Ford; and Congressman John C. Watts, who died in 1971.

In the prominent "pillow" position are "Uncle Sam" and the U.S.S.R. atop globes of the world, in opposing corners; but between the two she's placed the Rev. Ford Philpot with a Bible and the 23rd Psalm as her message of hope.

All this started from simply being given some scraps left from custom made shirting materials (probably from Graves Cox men's store since Harold Howard is there with his scissors and tape measure above the prestigious store label.)

Photo # 197 Courtesy Kevin Marc Florence, Lexington, Ky.

Photo # 198

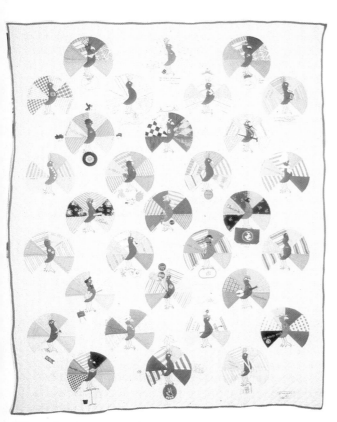

Photo # 199, 200, 201 Courtesy Mr. and Mrs. Harold Clem,
Nicholasville, Ky.

1950 - 1979

Photo # 202

Design: Spanish . . . (Something)
Type: Cross stitch
Size: 80″ x 95″
Maker: Rosemary Cox
Date: 1974
Condition: Excellent
Quilting: Straight line; feathered leaves
Value: $275.00 - $375.00

Comments: This is a Paragon Company kit bought at O'Neils Department Store, Akron, Ohio, but Rosemary has forgotten the exact name of the quilt. This brings up the point that, where names of patterns are known, they, too, should be included on the linen tag on the backs of quilts along with the quilter's name and the date the quilt was made. This quilt is dated and signed on the back.

Photo # 203

Design: Williamstown
Type: Cross stitch
Size: 80″ x 96″
Maker: Fannie Rose, Owen County, Kentucky
Date: c. 1974
Condition: Excellent
Quilting: Straight line; feathered leaves; fleurettes
Value: $275.00 - $375.00

Comments: This, too, is believed to be a Paragon Company pattern which was bought as a kit in a department store.

Cross stitched quilts are seen on the market for as little as $125.00 and as much as $400.00. They don't sell as well as do patchwork quilts but are often admired by the housewife for use in her decorating schemes. As far as I can determine, they are not yet "collectible" as a separate type of quilt.

Photo # 204

Design: Dogwood
Type: Applique
Size: 75″ x 93″
Maker: Marie Spicer Lucas, Lexington, Ky.
Date: c. 1978
Condition: Excellent
Quilting: Straight line
Value: $300.00 - $400.00

Comments: This is a kit quilt in a popular Dogwood design. The lady who made it has been sewing since she was a youngster placed in an orphan's home (1908) where they were required to spend a certain amount of time mending their own clothes and those of the smaller children.

Photo # 205

Design: Iris
Type: Applique
Size: 75″ x 89″
Maker: Alice Hudson, Owen County, Kentucky
Date: c. 1977
Condition: Excellent
Quilting: Straight line; cable
Value: $350.00 - $500.00

Comments: This is a Paragon kit quilt, one dearly loved by quilters since I have seen three hanging in various shows I've attended in the last six months. If you stand and listen to the viewer's comments, you find the pattern very well received!

The popularity of this quilt contributes to a rise in price above what is normally seen in present-day kit quilts. Generally speaking, they sell between $275.00 and $400.00.

Photo # 202 Courtesy Rosemary Cox, Uniontown, Ohio

Photo # 203 Courtesy Mr. and Mrs. Arvin Rose, Owenton, Ky.

Photo # 204 Courtesy of Mrs. Marie Lucas, Lexington, Ky.

Photo # 205 Courtesy Mr. and Mrs. Arvin Rose,
Owenton, Ky.

123

1950 - 1979

Photo # 206

Design: Log Cabin (Light and dark configuration)
Type: Patchwork
Size: 83" x 104"
Maker: Helen Marshall
Date: c. 1975
Condition: Excellent
Quilting: Not applicable
Value: $600.00 - $850.00

Comments: This quilt and the one following were made by sisters from fabrics taken from the same bolts of cloth. Each sister took her portion of the fabric and went her separate way to make the quilt. When they got together again to "compare," it was discovered that in one the pink coloring is predominant and in the other, the green seems to stand out. They say this exactly reflects their personal color choices and to a degree, their personalities.

I found it interesting because we're always SAYING that no two people will ever make a quilt exactly alike -- even given the same materials to use. Here, that is graphically illustrated.

Photo # 207

Design: Log Cabin (Light and dark configuration)
Type: Patchwork
Size: 85½" x 103"
Maker: Joy Newman
Date: c. 1975
Condition: Excellent
Quilting: Not applicable
Value: $600.00 - $850.00

Photo # 208

Design: Log Cabin (Light and dark with double diamond configuration)
Type: Patchwork
Size: 84" x 106"
Maker: Helen Marshall
Date: c. 1976
Condition: Excellent
Quilting: Not applicable
Value: $750.00 - $1,000.00

Comments: The maker has managed to combine two Log Cabin designs into one whole, thereby intensifying the interest the quilt generates.

Photo # 209

Design: Log Cabin (Combination of Straight Furrow and Streak of Lightning configuration)
Type: Patchwork
Size: 90" x 104"
Date: 1983
Condition: Excellent
Quilting: Outline
Value: $800.00 - $1,200.00

Comments: This quilt has been constructed entirely of Laura Ashley printed fabrics. (Laura Ashley is an English designer who started printing her own designs in a shoe-string operation in the middle fifties and who is now internationally known for her line of fabric designs.) No one can predict with any certainty, of course, but a hundred years from now, this quilt may be ultra-collectible just because of the Laura Ashley fabrics used in its construction. It, again, is a sign of the times in which it was made -- a quilt with "designer" fabrics, so to speak.

The quilt isn't hurt, either, by the intricate design of the Log Cabin patches suggesting both the Straight Furrow and the Zig-Zag or Streak of Lightning design.

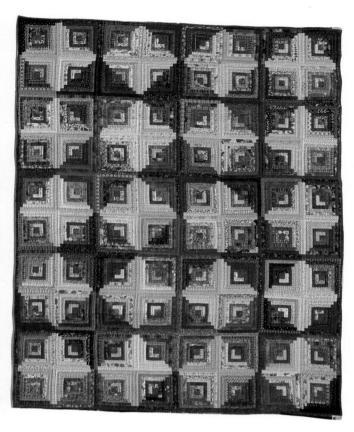

Photo # 206 Courtesy Mr. and Mrs. Robert Marshall, Doylestown, Ohio

Photo # 207 Courtesy Mr. and Mrs. Bill Newman, Ashland, Ohio

Photo # 208 Courtesy Mr. and Mrs. Robert Marshall, Doylestown, Ohio

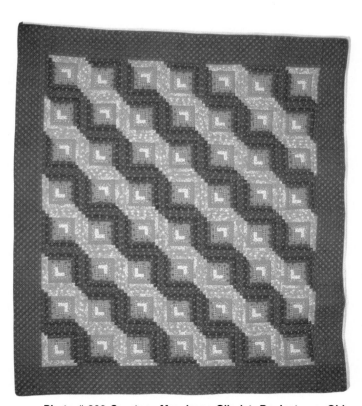

Photo # 209 Courtesy Mrs. Irene Gilcrist, Doylestown, Ohio

125

Photo # 210

Design: **Sampler**
Type: Applique
Size: 90″ x 102″
Maker: Mr. and Mrs. Allard's six children
Date: 1973
Condition: Excellent
Quilting: Outline; diagonal line
Value: $900.00 - $1,200.00

Comments: For a Christmas surprise, the Allard's children (living in six different states) decided to make their parents a quilt filled with loving memories of their family life together. Each wrote down a list of memories they'd like to see "done" and then, via phone and written notes, they chose which blocks they'd like to make themselves. The blocks were "laid out" at Thanksgiving and the quilt finished before Christmas.

The family home is here; so is gardening, canning, Christmas tree felling, games at the card table; swimming, etc. Rubbing her hand in a caressing gesture across the face of the quilt, Mrs. Allard said quietly, "I enjoy using it. It makes me think of each one!" There is a wealth of love in that statement, as there is in this quilt. It's visibly there.

One of her children you'll probably know. She's Linda Allard, the New York fashion designer.

Photo # 210 Courtesy Mr. and Mrs. Carroll Allard, Doylestown, Ohio

Photo # 211

Design: Pineapple
Type: Patchwork
Size: 86″ x 106″
Maker: Audrey Humphrey
Date: July, 1976
Condition: Excellent
Quilting: Outline, hearts, waving border
Value: $275.00 - $450.00

Comments: This is the first quilt Audrey attempted. She said she only found out later that this is considered one of the hardest patterns to make. She picked it out because she liked it.
One of the reasons the quilting shows up so well is because it has been quilted in contrasting thread.

Photo # 212

Design: Storm at Sea
Type: Patchwork
Size: 84″ x 85″
Maker: Audrey Humphrey
Date: February, 1980
Condition: Excellent
Quilting: Outline
Value: $300.00 - $450.00

Photo # 213

Design: Laced Star (Starry Path, Twisted Star, Tangled Star)
Type: Patchwork
Size: 60″ x 73″
Maker: Audrey Humphrey
Date: 1983
Condition: Excellent
Quilting: Outline and diagonal line
Value: $275.00 - $425.00

Photo # 214

Design: Saturn and Stars
Type: Applique
Size: 69″ x 82″
Maker: Audrey Humphrey
Date: 1982
Condition: Excellent
Quilting: Diamonds
Value: $450.00 - $600.00

Comments: Audrey says the idea for this quilt came from one she saw pictured in a magazine; however, as quilters are wont to do, she changed the design a bit to suit her own taste.
Since that first quilt in July of 1976, she has made in the neighborhood of 38 quilts! She is typical of today's quilters in that she is young and her quilting travels with her to do at odd moments of leisure. That's a bit like the colonial woman and her "pocket" in which were held her needle, thread and scissors. It was tied around her waist and hung in the folds of her dress so that she, too, was ready to sew at a moment's leisure. Idle hands were considered to be "the devil's workshop."

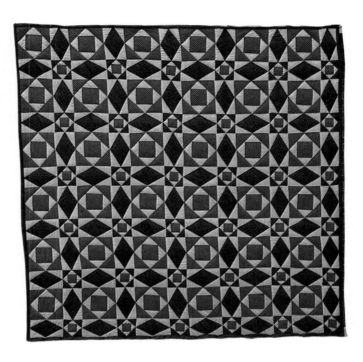

Photo # 212 Courtesy Audrey Humphrey, Kent, Ohio

Photo # 211 Courtesy Audrey Humphrey, Kent, Ohio

Photo # 213 Courtesy Audrey Humphrey, Kent, Ohio

Photo # 214 Courtesy Audrey Humphrey, Kent, Ohio

129

1979 - 1984

Photo # 215

Design: **Ohio Star** (Enlarged)
Type: Patchwork, Applique and Embroidery
Size: 83″ x 102″
Maker: Unknown; Tennessee
Date: c. 1978
Condition: Excellent
Quilting: Various motifs, zigzag, tulips
Value: $300.00 - $400.00

Comments: At first glance, this looks like an Evening Star design. However, it does have the middle diamond motif. Many of today's quilters are enlarging traditional patterns in this manner.

Photo # 216

Design: **Flowers of the Month**
Type: Patchwork and Embroidery
Size: 87″ x 103″
Maker: Lydia Ann Raber
Date: c. 1980
Condition: Excellent
Quilting: Diamonds and flowers
Value: $500.00 - $800.00

Comments: Mr. Ladd said he felt bad about buying this because the young Amish girl who made it cried when it had to be sold. I made a special effort to put this in the book -- for her. She'll probably never know that thousands can cherish her work because she had to give it up; but we'll know!

The flowers are done in satin stitch embroidery which makes them prominent enough to hold their own against the bold brown sashing and the Ice Cream Cone Border.

Photo # 217

Design: **Urn of Flowers**
Type: Applique
Size: 80″ x 100″
Maker: Hilda Kidwell, Godfrey, Illinois
Date: 1979
Condition: Excellent
Quilting: Diamond and straight line
Value: $1,350.00 - $1,750.00

Comments: This is a newly made applique in the style of an older one. The pattern was one shown in the Fall, 1983, issue of *McCall's Needlework & Crafts,* which was taken from a quilt made by Mrs. Susan McCord of McCordsville, Indiana, in the 1840's. When Hilda made her version, she exercised quilter's license and changed the direction of the urns.

Photo # 218

Design: **Missouri Daisy** (Golden Glow, Star Flower)
Size: 86″ x 104″
Date: c. 1978
Value: $325.00 - $425.00

Photo # 215 Courtesy Mr. and Mrs. John Davis, Acworth, Ga.

Photo # 216 Courtesy Mr. and Mrs. John Ladd, Doylestown, Oh

Photo # 217 Courtesy Spirit of America, St. Louis, Mo.

Photo # 218 Courtesy Edna Barnes, Uniontown, Ohio

Photo # 219

Design: Second Floor Window Next Door (Pieced Star, Star Puzzle and "Barbara Fritchie" Star)
Type: Patchwork and Applique
Size: 72" x 84"
Maker: William "Scooter" Poore
Date: 1979
Condition: Excellent
Quilting: Straight line; outline
Value: $750.00 - $1,000.00

Comments: (The shadow line is from an overhead electric wire and is not a part of the quilt.) This quilt is collectible for several reasons. First, it's an original design. Second, it's collectible for the design itself which is bold, masculine, eye-catching, filled with line and substance while at the same time managing to capture a delicacy of feeling in the rendering of the light and sky. Third, it's collectible BECAUSE it was made by a man. There are some who collect only those quilts made by men. It's considered a separate TYPE.

Photo # 220

Design: Log Cabin (Barn Raising and Squared Cross configurations)
Type: Patchwork
Size: 86" x 93½"
Maker: John Davis
Date: 1983
Condition: Excellent
Quilting: Outline
Value: $400.00 - $650.00

Comments: A contractor, Mr. Davis made this quilt as a way to relax during a particularly busy year building houses.

Notice how he created not one, but TWO designs by the arrangement of logs in the quilt. There's the traditional barn raising effect; but there is also a squared cross in the design.

Photo # 221

Design: Flying Geese
Type: Patchwork
Size: 92" x 114"
Date: 1982
Condition: Excellent
Quilting: Outline and chains
Value: $600.00 - $900.00

Comments: Using a traditional design, Dr. Levy sought a fabric that would create the illusion of "age." He found what he sought in a Jinny Beyer™ paisley print. By making the print bolder than the Flying Geese design, he furthered the aged effect by alluding to the older type of patchwork known as Roman Stripes.

His use of a nationally known designer's fabric adds to the value of this quilt as does his own wonderful sense of what is fitting in color and design. Again, the quilting was done by others to his specifications.

Photo # 222

Design: Amish Shadows
Type: Patchwork
Maker: Joseph Humphrey
Date: 1983
Condition: Excellent
Quilting: Commercial
Value: $250.00 - $350.00

Comments: Joe started quilting when his job of 14 years went by the wayside in the recent economic crunch. This is a kit quilt which he had commercially (machine) quilted. It's one of the few that I have ever seen that "worked." The flowers done in the black definitely add to this quilt and the border quilting has been well designed. Because it's commercially quilted, however, it will never have the monetary potential it could have achieved had he hand quilted it himself.

Photo # 220 Courtesy John Davis, Acworth, Ga.

Photo # 219 Courtesy William S. Poore, Seattle, Wash.

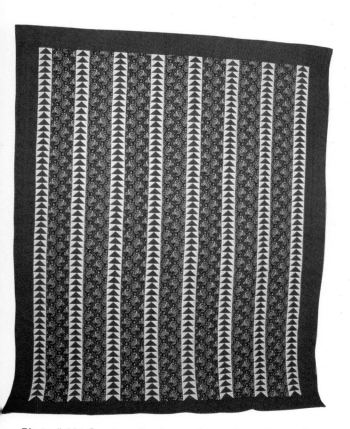

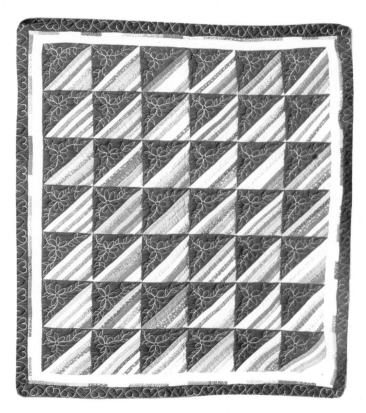

Photo # 221 Courtesy Dr. Jerome Levy, Creve Coeur, Mo.

Photo # 222 Courtesy Mr. Joseph Humphrey, Kent, Ohio

Photo # 223, 224

Design: Duck Pond
Type: Applique, Reverse Applique, Seminole Patchwork, Direct Dye and Batik Work
Size: 80″ x 100″
Maker: Rebecca Seigel
Date: 1982
Condition: Excellent
Quilting: Straight line; outline; contour; ''waves''; ''ducks''
Value: $2,500.00 - $3,500.00

Comments: Rebecca made this quilt after visiting Chincoteague, Va., which she says is the wild pony and duck decoy capital of the world!

Not content to employ general fabrics in her pond, she used a process of direct dye and batik work (painting cloth areas with wax, causing the fabric to resist the dye bath; once dry, the wax is removed by heating it.)

The dragonflies are applique and reverse applique work; the top ducks are batik; the fish and frogs are appliqued with embroidery fabric and dipped in a dye bath. (The fabric on the fish is little ducks!) The lillies are direct dye and reverse applique work.

This is the type of quilt that is an instant work of art and can only get better!

Photo # 225, 226

Design: Paper Doll Quilt
Type: Applique and Embroidery
Size: 66″ square
Maker: Rebecca Seigel
Condition: Excellent
Quilting: Straight line; outline; ''paper dolls''
Value: $2,200.00 - $3,000.00

Comments: Rebecca says she made this one for herself. She loved paper dolls as a child. She did this via a Zerox™ color transfer of an actual ''Diana Lynn'' doll. She then spent time in the Cincinnati library and museum, studying the fashions of the 1950's. Each of the costumes removes via velcro patches, revealing a doll clothed in her undies. Thus, you could actually ''play paper dolls' with this quilt!

When I visited Rebecca, I was struck by the old-world charm of her setting and the feeling of tranquility that pervades her home with its high ceilings and stencilled wall border. I was greeted by ducks and playful kittens and thought it must be a child's dream to be brought up here. I was shown her workroom and through her husband's shop. He's a potter. The entire place was alive with the creativity of its inhabitants. She had a section of a quilt design on her bulletin board that I can't wait to see finished!

Photo # 223, 224 Courtesy Rebecca Seigel, Owenton, Ky.

Photo # 225, 226 Courtesy Rebecca Seigel, Owenton, Ky.

Photo # 227

Design: Navajo Weaver (original copyrighted design)
Type: Patchwork and Applique
Maker: Susan Locher
Date: Fall, 1982
Condition: Excellent
Quilting: Outline; straight line
Value: $750.00 - $1,000.00

Comments: Susan got the idea for this quilt from a book on rugs. It's made of 100% cotton and was pieced by machine.

Photo # 228

Design: Presidential Seal
Type: Applique
Size: 85″ x 95″
Maker: Susan Locher
Date: 1983
Condition: Excellent
Quilting: Straight line; fan; circles
Value: $750.00 - $1,000.00

Comments: The inspiration for this design came from the back of a half dollar. Susan had to do some library research on the eagle before she attempted her drawing and ''feathering.''

Photo # 229

Design: Deco (original copyrighted design)
Type: Patchwork and Applique
Size: 85″ x 95″
Maker: Susan Locher
Date: 1983
Condition: Excellent
Quilting: Lines
Value: $750.00 - $1,000.00

Comments: This won second place in the annual O'Neil's Department Store Quilt Show in Akron, Ohio. It is done in silks and satins and was pieced by machine.

Photo # 227 Courtesy Susan Locher, Talmadge, Ohio

Photo # 228 Courtesy Susan Locher, Talmadge, Ohio

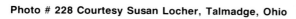

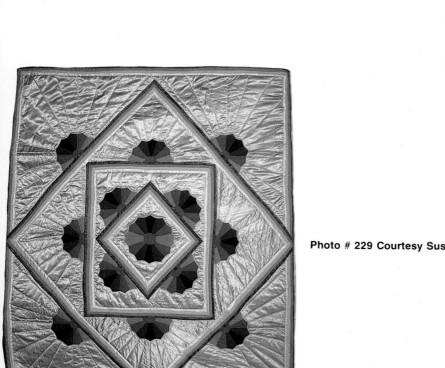

Photo # 229 Courtesy Susan Locher, Talmadge, Ohio

Photo # 230

Design: Public Square
Type: Ribbon Applique
Size: 106″ x 114″
Maker: Fran Soika
Date: 1980
Condition: Excellent
Quilting: Lines
Value: $2,500.00 - $2,700.00

Comments: This was adapted from a water color by her daughter, Judy. All pieces were basted to a foundation fabric and then appliqued permanently using ¼″ to ⅜″ ribbon.

Photo # 231

Design: Tunisian Wedding
Type: Applique and Reverse Applique
Size: 104″ x 121″
Maker: Fran Soika
Date: 1983
Condition: Excellent
Quilting: Contour, ¼″
Value: $2,800.00 - $3,200.00

Photo # 232

Design: The Nutcracker
Type: Applique
Size: 74″ x 94″
Maker: Fran Soika
Date: 1982
Condition: Excellent
Quilting: Contour, ¼″
Value: $2,500.00 - $3,000.00

Comments: This was made for a raffle for the Cleveland Ballet in 1982. It has fabrics from costume cuttings and shows five of the set designs. The snow effect was created by using a random black and white dot, on the right side for sky, on the wrong side for houses.

Photo # 233

Design: Coppelia
Type: Applique
Size: 49″ x 72″
Maker: Fran Soika
Date: 1983
Condition: Excellent
Quilting: Diamonds, straight line, and contour, ¼″
Value: $2,200.00 - $2,700.00

Comments: This was made for a Cleveland Ballet raffle. On the back of the quilt pertinent information was placed on the ribbons of ballet slippers. Her designs carry over to the back of her quilts.

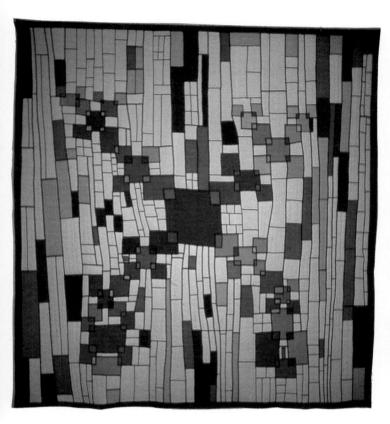

Photo # 230 Courtesy Fran Soika, Novelty, Ohio

Photo # 231 Courtesy Fran Soika, Novelty, Ohio

Photo # 232 Courtesy Fran Soika, Novelty, Ohio

Photo # 233 Courtesy Fran Soika, Novelty, Ohio

Photo # 234

Design: **Come Fly With Me**
Type: Applique
Size: 75″ x 92″
Maker: Fran Soika
Date: 1983
Condition: Excellent
Quilting: Contour, ¼″
Value: $2,800.00 - $3,300.00

Comments: This won the Judge's Choice award for contemporary design at the O'Neil's Quilt Show in 1983.
While doing this, she found it necessary to do some balloon flying; so she considered this to have been a "fun" quilt to do.

Photo # 235

Design: **The Cat**
Type: Patchwork and Applique
Size: 73″ x 79″
Maker: Fran Soika
Date: 1984
Condition: Excellent
Quilting: Diamonds; outline
Value: $2,700.00 - $3,200.00

Comments: This is the result of her yearly effort to produce one of Edward Larson's designs. He's a woodcarver and quilt designer from Libertyville, Illinois. This one she's keeping for her very own as she just couldn't give it up.

Photo # 234 Courtesy Fran Soika, Novelty, Ohio

Photo # 235 Courtesy Fran Soika,
Novelty, Ohio

Photo # 236

Design: Liberty Crown (original design by Wanda Davis)
Type: Patchwork
Size: 104″ x 105″
Maker: Wanda Davis, North Georgia
Date: 1983
Condition: Excellent
Quilting: Fleur de lis; medallions; scallops
Value: $450.00 - $700.00

Comments: The lady who made this said the more she worked on the design on her graph paper, the more it reminded her of the crown on the Statue of Liberty, so she called it Liberty Crown. We thought this a timely and fitting quilt to include, not only because it's a wonderful new design, but because of all the work and money going to refurbish the 100 year old Liberty. Quilt subjects and names are often reflective of the time in which they're made -- even today!

Photo # 237

Design: Sampler
Type: Patchwork and Applique
Size: 72″ x 91″
Maker: Emogene Gardner
Date: 1982
Condition: Excellent
Quilting: Outline
Value: $350.00 - $525.00

Comments: This quilt of sample patchwork designs and her grandson's precious handprint won the Kentucky Homemaker's Extension Award; won a blue ribbon at the Kentucky State Fair; and won first place at the Radcliff Quilt Show. Save for the sashing, its made entirely from scrap fabrics saved from family clothing. Notice that the Prairie Points around the border are also made from scraps.

Photo # 238, 239

Design: Oklahoma Heritage
Type: Patchwork and Applique
Size: 85″ square
Maker: Alice Schmude
Date: 1982
Condition: Excellent
Quilting: Diamonds
Value: $1,000.00 - $1,500.00

Comments: This was made to commemorate the 75th anniversary of Oklahoma's statehood. Mrs. Schmude's husband, Don, drew the design for the quilt, including the Indian applique.
    She machine pieced the star using the quick piecing method laid out in *The Lonestar Quilt Handbook* by Blanche and Helen Young. It is hand quilted.
    I am particularly impressed with the feathered Indian design lending itself so well to the Lone Star pattern and by the three dimensional effect given the center portion of the star by the mere choice of colors!

Photo # 236 Courtesy Mr. and Mrs. John Davis, Acworth, Ga.

Photo # 237 Courtesy Emogene Gardner, Hodgenville, Ky.

Photo # 238, 239 Courtesy Alice Schmude, Tulsa, Okla.

Photo # 240

Design: Shower Curtain (original)
Type: Applique
Size: 54½″ x 66″
Maker: Ami Simms
Date: 1982
Condition: Excellent
Quilting: Outline
Value: $250.00 - $350.00

Comments: Ami says everything behind her shower curtain looks like what's on it EXCEPT for the shark.

Photo # 241

Design: Sinking Ship (original)
Type: Patchwork
Size: 10″ x 31″
Maker: Ami Simms
Date: 1982
Condition: Excellent
Quilting: Diamonds; "waves"
Value: $75.00 - $125.00

Comments: This is what's known as a quilter's "joke," done to elicit a smile, which is exactly what happens at a show when it's set among all those "serious" quilts.

Photo # 242

Design: Amish Farmyard (original)
Type: Applique
Size: 23″ square
Maker: Ami Simms
Date: 1983
Condition: Excellent
Quilting: Straight line; contour
Value: $225.00 - $325.00

Comments: Youthful Ami owes her considerable skill (10/11 stitches per inch) to the happy occasion of being housed with an Amish family during her sojourn at college. "They were all gathered around the quilting frame in my sponsor mother's home when I arrived, and I asked what they were doing and ultimately, would they show me how; and they stopped what they were doing, taking hours away from their work to do so!" (It was certainly not a waste of their time!) This "picture" is of her Amish family's farm. She observed their reservations toward being photographed by having them face the barns rather than the viewer.
This design won a special recognition award at the Smokey Mountain Quilt Competition in 1983.

Photo # 240 Courtesy Ami Simms, Flint, Mich.

Photo # 241 Courtesy Ami Simms, Flint, Mich.

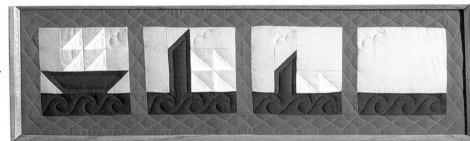

Photo # 242 Courtesy Ami Simms, Flint, Mich.

Photo # 243

Design: Joy
Type: Applique, Reverse and Ribbon Applique
Size: 35″ x 53″
Maker: Katie Couch
Date: 1982
Condition: Excellent
Quilting: Religious symbols
Value: $300.00 - $500.00

Comments: This was inspired by a Hallmark™ greeting card. Much of the quilting is symbolic of the story of Jesus. The light blue panels have gold thread and botanical representations of frankincense and myrrh, the gifts of the Magi. There are quilted lavender sand dollars and lillies. The center flower at the top is a passion flower. The rows of quilting around Mary's neck represents the necklaces of the Earth Mother. In the sky are 13 major stars, one without a halo (Judas.)

Photo # 244

Design: Lone Star
Type: Patchwork
Size: 86″ x 108″
Maker: Elizabeth Coblentz
Date: 1983
Condition: Excellent
Quilting: Diamonds; medallions
Value: $600.00 - $800.00

Comments: An Amish lady quilted this, but Rosie advised on the color layout. Rosie says she's learned "soooo much" from the Amish and that they're miles ahead of "us" when it comes to actual quilting. "Why, they can even quilt working away from themselves by just bobbing the needle up and down with their thumb!"

Photo # 245

Design: Beanstalk
Type: Applique
Size: 80½″ x 89½″
Maker: Caron L. Mosey
Date: 1983
Condition: Excellent
Quilting: Straight line; contour
Value: $2,500.00 - $3,500.00

Comments: Beanstalk was made for Caron's son, Loren, and went straight from her mind to the cloth. She made no templates or charts. She said she worked hardest on the sky portion, "trying to fashion the cloth to give the appearance of sky and cloud layers."

Photo # 246

Design: My Summer Window
Type: Applique "Stained Glass"
Size: 90″ x 108″
Maker: Marjorie Sanders
Date: 1983
Condition: Excellent
Quilting: Ribbon Applique
Value: $1,250.00 - $1,750.00

Comments: This was inspired by having looked at a stained glass quilt pattern book and being caught in a Montana meadow in a rain storm. After the storm, Marjorie was struck by the wonder of her natural surroundings, arched by a lovely rainbow and encompassed by field flowers. As simply as that, an idea for a quilt was born!

The rainbow is bias tape; the silver lined cloud is a metallic fabric; the window area is polyester chiffon with black bias tape serving as "leading." Flowers are all polyester satin bound with black bias tape; and the binding has four layers of batting to give the "framed" look she desired.

Photo # 243 Courtesy Katie Couch, San Jose, Calif.

Photo # 244 Courtesy Rosie Wade, Marietta, Ga.

Photo # 245 Courtesy Caron L. Mosey, Flushing, Mich.

Photo # 246 Courtesy Majorie Sanders,
Cloverleaf Quilts, Kalispell, Mont.

Photo # 247

Design: Hmong Stitchery
Type: Patchwork and Reverse Applique
Size: 94″ square
Maker: Chee Vang
Date: c. 1983
Condition: Excellent
Quilting: Not applicable
Value: $425.00 - $625.00

Comments: A book on quilts would not be complete without mentioning the work of the Hmong ("boat people" from Laos) who have settled in our country and are selling their exquisite handwork as a means of livelihood. In place of wedding collars, pouches, money belts and sashes, they're making potholders, placemats and larger bed spreads. In their culture, a girl started learning the tiny stitches at nine years of age, knowing that her skill would be a measure of her value as a bride. Here, values change. A child is quick to learn American ways and to specialize in how NOT to be "different." Learning pa ndau stitchery is not high on a young girl's list of things to do. There is concern that this beautiful stitchery will cease with the older generation.

I watched a Laotian lady work on a piece at a mall. She held two fabrics together, one atop the other, scored the top into tiny squares with her needle in a design that was only seen in her mind's eye. Then she lifted off certain of the scored squares revealing the rich color of the contrasting fabric beneath. Next, she started binding the two fabrics together with the tiniest stitching, carefully tucking the edge under with ever increasing number of stitches. (She did this all while watching a small child and helping customers who came to her booth.) You could scarcely see where she had stitched. They were all "hidden." It looked as if that fabric had decided to roll itself under like that!

Photo # 248

Design: Hershel Walker
Type: Applique
Maker: Rosie Wade
Date: 1983
Condition: Excellent
Quilting: Straight line; contour
Value: Undetermined

Comments: Mrs. Wade drew this free hand from a picture she saw in *Sports Illustrated* at the suggestion of her husband who thought it would make a neat quilt! (Need I say he's a football fan?) Notice her splendid use of fabrics to create the illusion of crowds and speed. She says she's very grateful to Chris Wolf Edmonds who taught a workshop on faces and to her mother who joined a quilting club at a Baptist church!

She sent the quilt to Mr. Walker who liked it and autographed it for her on May 13, 1983. In that, she carries forward a long standing tradition. Ladies from the 1840s to the 1930's used to send fabrics (or request personal fabrics from famous personalities of the time) to have them autographed. Surviving examples of these are found with names like "Lincoln," "Grant," "Greenaway," "Roosevelt," "Pickford," and other notables of the time. These quilts are VERY collectible!

This quilt won the sports category at the Quilt Georgia show in Savannah in 1983.

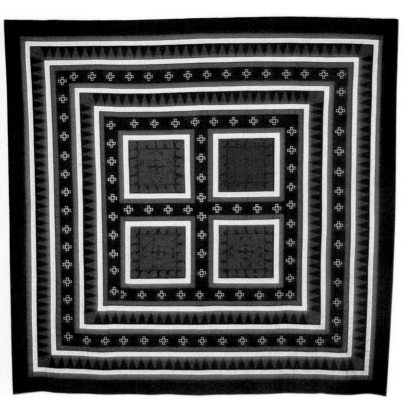

Photo # 247

Photo # 248 Courtesy Rosie Wade, Marietta, Ga.

1979 - 1984

Photo # 249

Design: State Flower
Type: Applique
Size: 74″ x 88″
Maker: Emma Roberts, Dayton, Ohio
Value: $300.00 - $400.00

Comments: Mrs. Roberts has made over 60 quilts in her lifetime and has given them all away as gifts.

Photo # 250

Design: Map Quilt
Type: Patchwork and Embroidery
Size: 94″ x 108″
Maker: Susan Yoder
Date: 1978 - 1982
Condition: Excellent
Quilting: Straight line, feather border, hearts, etc.
Value: $500.00 - $850.00

Comments: Each of the states is outlined, has the official state flower and bird and tells when that state entered the union and in what position. This was made by an Amish girl and it is referred to in their circles as an ''educational'' quilt. (Your history lesson comes with your embroidery needle.) This is a traditional way of teaching girls, one used 200 years ago; only then, they worked samplers filled with elaborate embroidery stitches which they kept to ''remind'' them how to do the intricate stitches later in life.

Photo # 251

Design: Rocking Horse
Type: Stencil
Date: 1984
Condition: Excellent
Quilting: Tied
Value: $75.00 - $100.00

Comments: I wanted to show a present-day stencil quilt and this seemed a charming example. Stencilling was carried on in the mid 1840's but surviving examples from this time frame in any condition are rarely seen. I ran into one on the market dated in the late 1840s, in excellent condition, and signed by the maker. The asking price was $7,500.00. The art of stencilling designs has only recently been revived as a result of the interest in crafts generated in part by the Bicentennial celebrations in 1976! It's interesting to note that around each celebration of our country's birth (1876, 1926, 1976) there's been a revived interest in quilting and hand crafted items.

Those marvelous wooden toys were hand-made by Dick Showalter, Sunshine Toys, McKenzie Bridge, Oregon.

The blue doll coverlet is a Dollie Stevens, 15″ x 22″, and is worth $75.00 - $125.00. (A long time ago, the coverlets came WITH the dolls.)

Photo # 252

Design: Scandinavian Peasant
Type: Applique
Maker: Karen Drake
Date: 1983
Condition: Excellent
Quilting: Diamonds
Value: Asking $3,000.00

Comments: This is a beautifully executed kit quilt.

Photo # 249 Courtesy Mr. and Mrs. Jerry Zwisler, Englewood, Ohio

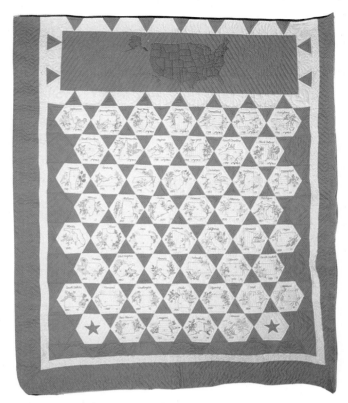

Photo # 250 Courtesy Mr. and Mrs. John Ladd, Doylestown, Ohio

Photo # 251 Courtesy Mr. and Mrs. Allen Showalter, Doylestown, Ohio

Photo # 252 Courtesy Karen Drake, Ohio

Photo # 253

Design: Bride's Quilt - Baltimore Style (Kit design by Pat Cox)
Type: Applique
Size: 96″ square
Maker: Bernice Enyeart, Professional Quilter
Date: 1983
Condition: Excellent
Quilting: Basket weave design
Value: Insured at $10,000.00

Comments: This quilt won the prestigious Best In Show award at the 14th annual National Quilting Association Quilt Show held in Bell Buckle, Tennessee, in August of 1983.

Over 1,800 hours in the making, it was made from a kit design based on the 1840's Baltimore Album quilts and it is exquisite!

Photo # 253 Courtesy Bernice Enyeart, Huntington, Ind., Photograph by Myron Miller, New York

Photo # 254

Design: **Hole in the Barn Door** (Monkey Wrench, Double Monkey Wrench, Shoo-fly, Sherman's March, Puss-in-the-Corner, Love Knot, Lincoln's Platform, Churn Dash)
Size: 68″ x 78″
Maker: Mrs. Emmanuel Swartzentruber
Condition: Good; binding needs to be eased
Value: $400.00 - $600.00

Photo # 255

Design: **Four Patch Chains**
Size: 68″ x 73″
Maker: Sarah and Mary Miller
Date: 1981
Value: $350.00 - $500.00

Comments: The makers were forced to sell this when their barn met with catastrophy and had to be replaced.

Photo # 256

Design: **Philadelphia Pavement Variation**
Size: 33″ x 37″ wallhanging
Maker: Lavina Swartzentruber
Value: $125.00 - $200.00

Photo # 257

Design: **Diamond Star Log Cabin** (original)
Size: 90″ x 105″
Maker: Verna Klein
Date: 1982
Value: $650.00 - $800.00

Comments: Amish quilts, such as these four, command very high prices with some collectors and in some states, namely Pennsylvania, Ohio, Massachusetts and Indiana. I'm told that even tattered ones were bringing $800.00 at the last Brimfield flea market; and I know that there are avid collectors for them on both coasts. Very graphic and otherwise outstanding examples from some select old order Amish sects have reportedly sold to collectors for as much as $7,500.00. However, since I'm reporting here all I was able to learn in this last frenetic year, I'm compelled to say that three different dealers (well known, well traveled and well respected) have voluntarily told me that they won't buy Amish quilts unless they know they've a show coming up in one of the above states. To quote, "southern people don't like the drab colors and won't buy them. I just waste my time and space carrying them to shows out of those four state areas."

At least three new books have recently been pubished on Amish quilts; so perhaps this will stimulate a more amenable general market.

Photo # 254 Courtesy Mr. and Mrs. John Ladd,
Doylestown, Ohio

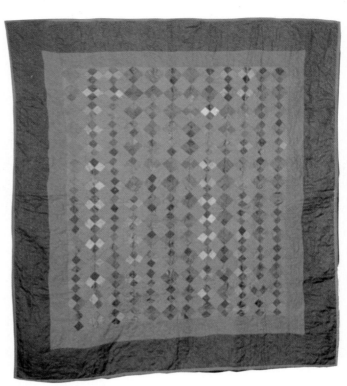

Photo # 255 Courtesy Mr. and Mrs. John Ladd, Doylestown, Ohio

Photo # 256 Courtesy Mr. and Mrs. John Ladd,
Doylestown, Ohio

Photo # 257

Baskets

Photo # 258

Design: Basket of Flowers
Size: 74½" x 75"
Maker: Unknown; Indiana
Date: c. 1935
Value: $275.00 - $400.00

Comments: This quilt was supposed to have a flower applique drooping over the side. Had there been five triangles across and down instead of six, the design would have been Cherry Basket.

Photo # 259

Design: Basket of Fruit
Maker: Unknown; Texas
Date: c. 1935
Condition: Some "boxing" stains
Quilting: Runing vine leaves
Value: $300.00 - $450.00

Photo # 260

Design: Basket of Lillies (Basket of Flowers)
Size: 90" x 102"
Date: c. 1935
Quilting: Fleur de lis, 12 stitches per inch; Swag and Tassle border
Value: $500.00 - $750.00

Photo # 261

Design: Grandmother's Basket of Flowers
Size: 87" x 89"
Date: c. 1935
Value: $450.00 - $650.00

Comments: This quilt has a rick rack border (smaller) which was revived in the 1930's, mostly in kits.

Photo # 258 Courtesy Rich Norton, Noblesville, Ind.

Photo # 259 Courtesy Harry and Anita Wood, Odessa, Texas

Photo # 260 Courtesy James Young, Nashville Flea Market

Photo # 261 Courtesy Rick Norton, Noblesville, Ind.

Baskets

Photo # 262

Design: Cake Stand
Size: 60″ x 84″
Maker: Unknown: Illinois
Date: c. 1885
Value: $125.00 - $175.00

Photo # 263

Design: Urn of Flowers or Sugar Bowl
Type: Applique
Size: 73″ x 87″
Maker: Unknown: Ohio
Date: c. 1890
Quilting: Quarter circle
Value: $250.00 - $375.00

Comments: The names are "word of mouth" names from old time quilters. I can't document either! The "flowers" have been machine appliqued in contrasting thread so they'll be noticed. The quarter circle quilting motif is called "shell" by old timers and "fan" by modern writers.

Photo # 264

Design: Flower Pot
Size: 66″ x 73″
Date: c. 1935
Quilting: 1″ square
Value: $200.00 - $300.00

Comments: Notice the border treatment. Too many quilters disregard pieced borders. They can "make" a quilt!

Photo # 265

Design: Flower Basket
Size: 71″ x 91″
Maker: Unknown: Indiana
Date: c. 1900
Quilting: Tied
Value: $95.00 - $125.00

Comments: A wool comfort, blue and pink cotton sateen backing. "Signed" with someone's embroidered symbol.

Photo # 262

Photo # 263 Courtesy Marcel Ulrich, McDonald, Ohio

Photo # 264

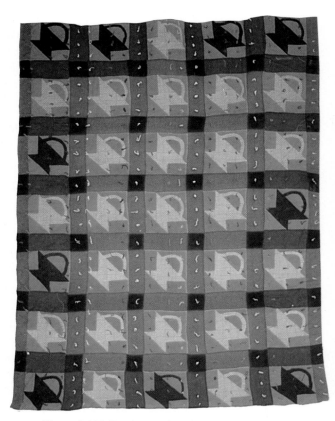

Photo # 265 Purchased from Mary Pharr, Sullivan, Ind.

159

Chains

Photo # 266

Design: Nine Patch Plaid
Size: 69" x 84"
Date: c. 1890
Condition: Frayed head binding
Quilting: ½" diamond
Value: $250.00 - $350.00

Comments: Made of shirting fabrics.

Photo # 267

Design: Double Irish Chain
Size: 66" x 74"
Date: c. 1890
Value: $350.00 - $450.00

Comments: Blue and white star print fabric.

Photo # 268

Design: Double Irish Chain
Date: c. 1930
Value: $300.00 - $400.00

Photo # 269

Design: Triple Irish Chain
Size: 61½" x 82"
Maker: Unknown; Indiana
Date: c. 1890
Value: $225.00 - $300.00

Comments: Made from shirting fabrics, cotton seed batting.

Photo # 270

Design: Twist Patchwork (Godey's Design, 1851; Kansas Dugout, 1942; Ribbon Twist, Plaited Block)
Size: 63½" x 73½"
Maker: Unknown: Indiana
Date: c. 1895
Value: $125.00 - $200.00

Photo # 271

Design: Federal Chain
Size: 72" x 78"
Maker: Kathryn Fritz Bugger, O'Fallon, Illinois
Date: c. 1900-1910
Value: $1,200.00 - $1,500.00

Comments: All cotton quilt.

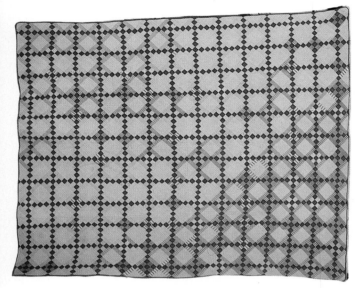

Photo # 266 Courtesy Helen Van Zant,
Washington Court House, Ohio

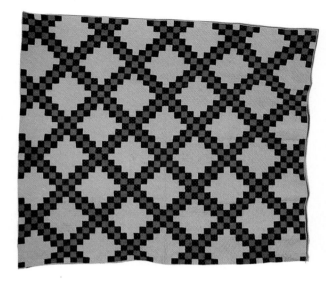

Photo # 267 Courtesy Alice Warobiew, Brookfield, Ohio

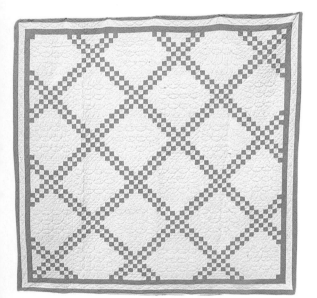

Photo # 268 Courtesy Alice Warobiew, Brookfield, Ohio

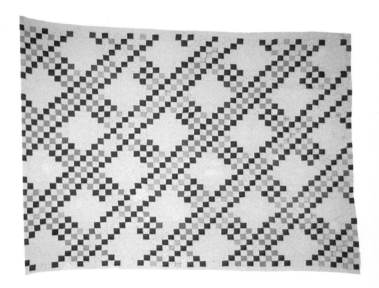

Photo # 269

Photo # 270

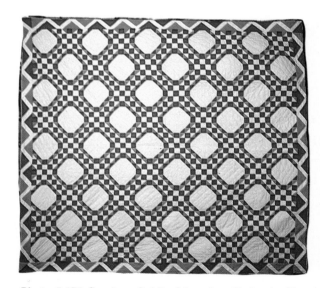

Photo # 271 Courtesy Spirit of America, St. Louis, Mo.

161

Fans

Photo # 272

Design: **Jacob's Fan** (combination Jacob's Ladder and Fan)
Size: 101″ x 102″
Date: Modern
Value: $400.00 - $600.00

Photo # 273

Design: **Peacock Fan**
Maker: Effie Lawrence
Date: c. 1920
Value: $225.00 - $300.00

Photo # 274

Design: **Mohawk Trail**
Size: 76″ x 90″
Date: c. 1975
Value: $225.00 - $300.00

Photo # 275

Design: **Baby Bunting**
Size: 77″ x 92½″
Maker: Alta Miller family (Mennonites); Indiana
Date: c. 1940
Value: $350.00 - $450.00

Photo # 272 Courtesy Mr. and Mrs. John Davis, Acworth, Ga.

Photo # 273 Courtesy Mr. and Mrs. Atwood Ayers, Owenton, Ky.

Photo # 274 Courtesy Rosemary Cox, Uniontown, Ohio

Photo # 275 Purchased from Eugene Rappaport, Centerville, Ind.

Geometric

Photo # 276

Design: Setting Sun Variation
Type: Patchwork
Size: 64½" square
Maker: Susan Maria Earle, (patches, c. 1850), New England; Flora Prouty Boyd Smith, (bought and cut sashing, 1928), Pennsylvania; Harriet Boyd Penrose (sewed it together, 1984), Kentucky
Condition: Excellent
Quilting: Circles, done by Sue Heidenreich, Lexington, 1984
Value: $350.00 - $500.00

Comments: This is a ''family'' quilt if there ever was one! It took great-grandmother, mother and child 134 years to get it finished. They have the original pattern (a sheet of thin paper with miniscule printing) and a sheet of paper with each generation's handwriting telling who passed the pieces to whom.

Photo # 277

Design: Spider Web String Quilt
Date: Modern
Quilting: Hand quilted July 1980
Value: $275.00 - $350.00

Photo # 278

Design: Nine Patch (Four Leaf Clover)
Date: c. 1980
Value: $250.00 - $325.00

Photo # 279

Design: Pyrotechnics Variation
Size: 77½" x 83"
Maker: Unknown: Ohio
Date: c. 1890
Quilting: Huge feathered medallion, 11 stitches per inch
Value: $300.00 - $450.00

Comments: Two short arms in the star make this a variation. Word-of-mouth name suggested was Ohio Compass, so I cannot document the true name. The green fabric with tiny brown dots was probably placed here in an ''obvious flaw'' attempt.

Photo # 280

Design: Pickle Dish (similar to Indian Wedding Ring)
Size: 80" x 93"
Date: c. 1935
Quilting: Nice
Value: $325.00 - $425.00

Photo # 281

Design: Wagon Wheels
Size: 68" x 75"
Date: c. 1955
Quilting: Circular, 1" apart
Value: $225.00 - $300.00

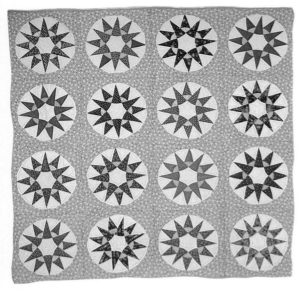

Photo # 276 Courtesy Harriet Penrose, Lexington, Ky.

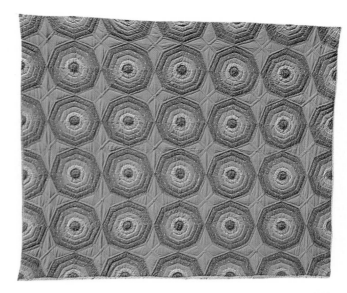

Photo # 277 Courtesy Audrey Humphrey, Kent, Ohio

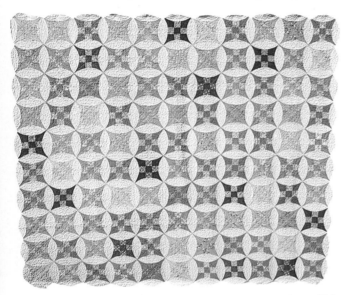

Photo # 278 Courtesy Joseph Humphrey, Kent, Ohio

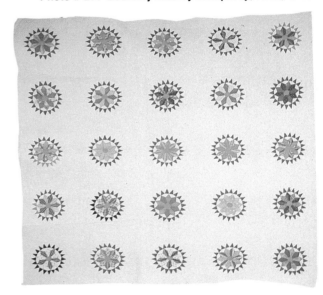

Photo # 279

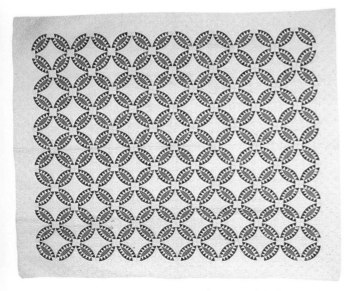

Photo # 280 Purchased from Joan Townsend, Lebanon, Ohio

Photo # 281

165

Geometric

Photo # 282

Design: Brick Wall
Size: 63″ x 77″
Maker: Unknown: Ohio
Date: c. 1910
Value: $60.00 - $90.00

Photo # 283

Design: London Stairs
Size: 72″ x 96″
Date: c. 1935
Quilting: 1″ square; unwashed
Value: $225.00 - $300.00

Photo # 284

Design: Herringbone
Maker: Mrs. Thomas (Hattie) Sherman Smith, Asher, Oklahoma
Date: c. 1930
Value: $250.00 - $350.00

Photo # 285

Design: Lady of the Lake
Size: 71½″ x 76″
Maker: Unknown: Lancaster, Pennsylvania
Date: c. 1950
Quilting: Urns, lyres, pineapples
Value: $300.00 - $425.00

Photo # 286

Design: Old Maid's Ramble
Size: 58½″ x 81½″
Date: c. 1910
Condition: Unwashed
Value: $350.00 - $450.00

Photo # 287

Design: London Square
Size: 63″ x 76″
Date: c. 1910
Condition: Rebound
Value: $150.00 - $225.00

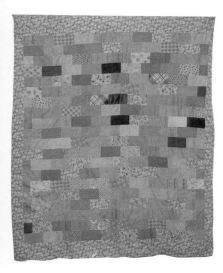

Photo # 282 Courtesy Joy Newman,
Ashland, Ohio

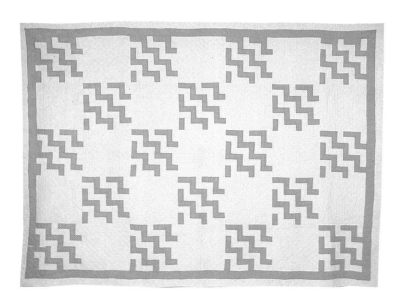

Photo # 283

Photo # 284
Courtesy Mr. and Mrs. Dowden Koerninger,
Sundown, Texas

Photo # 285 Courtesy Bill and Bunny Nolt, Worthington, Ohio

Photo # 286

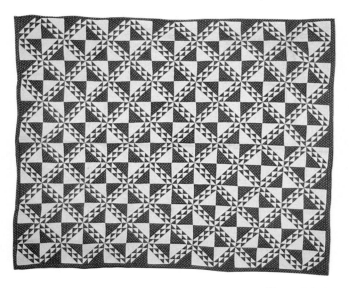

Photo # 287

167

Houses

Photo # 288

Design: **Red School House**
Size: 80″ x 99″
Maker: Unknown: Hamilton County, Indiana
Date: c. 1915
Condition: Some foxing, "obvious flaw"
Quilting: Diamonds, medallions and circles; 10 stitches per inch
Value: $2,000.00 - $3,000.00

Photo # 289

Design: **Old Kentucky Home**
Size: 84″ square
Date: c. 1910
Quilting: Circular and outline; 8 stitches per inch
Value: $750.00 - $1,000.00

Comments: Blue and white dot fabric, muslin backing, 18 houses.

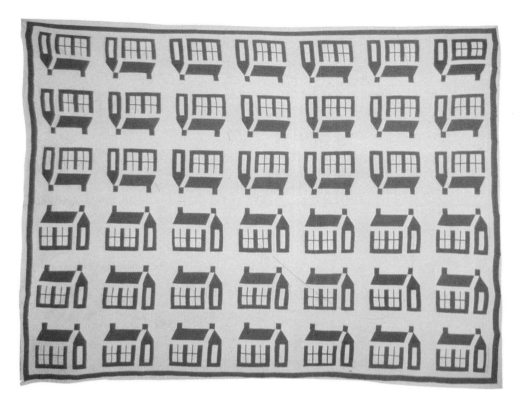

Photo # 288 Privately owned

Photo # 289 Courtesy Leo Walter, Stagecoach Antiques, Akron, Ohio

Mosaics

Photo # 290

Design: Field of Diamonds
Size: 68″ x 84″
Maker: Ginny ''Belle'' Cox, West Virginia
Date: c. 1938
Value: $125.00 - $200.00

Comments: This quilt has a red Garden Walk or Pathway manner of setting the block together. This pattern is called Rainbow Tile if there are only two rows of hexagons from center; it's Martha Washington's Garden if the ending three ''point'' hexagons are in like material.

Photo # 291

Design: Flower Garden (French Bouquet, Honeycomb, Mosaic, Grandmother's Flower Garden)
Size: 78″ x 80″
Maker: Unknown: Champaign, Illinois
Date: c. 1960
Value: $400.00 - $500.00

Comments: Satin materials back and front (called ''silks'' as in racing silks). This type pattern is called Garden Walk, Old Fashioned Flower Garden and Martha Washington's Flower Garden when it has three rows of hexagons surrounding the center.

Photo # 292

Design: Flower Garden
Size: 73″ x 79″
Maker: Florence Hodgson, Hollister, Ohio
Quilting: 10 stitches per inch
Value: $300.00 - $400.00

Comments: Interesting mosaic border.

Photo # 293

Design: Hexagonal Snow Garden
Type: Pieced
Size: 89″ x 90″
Maker: Piecing by Arlene Gugger; quilting by her mother, Adele Oldenettel, Bunker Hill, Illinois
Date: c. 1939-1940
Condition: An outstanding quilt
Value: $1,750.00 - $2,000.00

Comments: This quilt contains 25,000 pieces, each about ½″ wide.

Photo # 290 Courtesy Rosemary Cox, Uniontown, Ohio

Photo # 291

Photo # 292

Photo # 293 Courtesy Spirit of America, St. Louis, Mo.

Drunkard's Path

Photo # 294

Design: **Drunkard's Path** (Vine of Friendship)
Size: 64″ x 75″
Maker: Unknown, possibly a child as there are ''birds'' in the design and three blocks are backwards
Value: $150.00 - $225.00

Photo # 295

Design: **Drunkard's Path** (Solomon's Puzzle; Rocky Road to Dublin -- before 1849; Rocky Road to California; Country Husband)
Size: 69½″ x 76″
Maker: Unknown: Ohio
Date: c. 1910
Quilting: 1/8″ apart
Value: $250.00 - $350.00

Photo # 296

Design: **Drunkard's Path** and Unknown Pattern (possibly original)
Size: 72″ x 89″
Condition: Machine edged, frail
Value: $125.00 - $200.00

Comments: It's a bit like Cross and Crown, Easy Ways, Lily and Texas Flower or Texas Treasure; but it's not quite any of those. I suspect there's some quilter's message here, either religious, temperance-oriented or personal (i.e., she married a drunkard from Texas?)

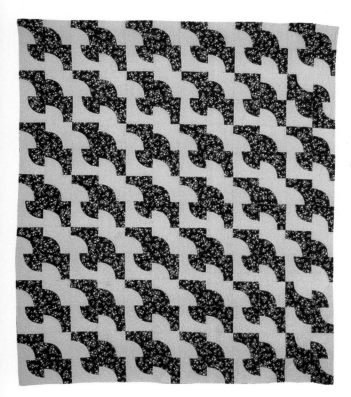

Photo # 294 Purchased at Georgetown Antique Mall, Georgetown, Ky.

Photo # 295 Courtesy Mrs. Arlene Showalter, Doylestown, Ohio

Photo # 296

Log Cabin

Photo # 297

      Design: **Straight Furrow** (Falling Timbers)
        Type: Tied comfort
        Size: 70″ x 77″
        Date: c. 1910
    Material: Gray flannel backing, cotton and wool fabrics, wool stuffing
       Value: $50.00 - $100.00

Photo # 298

      Design: **Courthouse Steps** (Capitol Steps)
        Type: Tied comfort
        Size: 69″ x 76″
        Date: c. 1900
  Condition: Some moth damage
    Material: Green, red and gray wool top, brown cotton backing with sprigged design
       Value: $100.00 - $150.00

Photo # 299

      Design: **Zig Zag**
        Size: 71½″ x 81″
        Date: c. 1890
    Material: Wool top, blue cotton backing, no stuffing
    Quilting: Feathered quilting in border
       Value: $350.00 - $500.00

Photo # 300

      Design: **Zig Zag**
        Maker: Unknown; Ohio
        Date: c. 1900
  Condition: Slight moth damage
    Material: Purple cotton sateen backing
       Value: $225.00 - $300.00

  Comments: English pleating technique makes this pattern look more like logs.

Photo # 301

      Design: **Chestnur Burr** (Windmill Blades)
        Size: 62″ x 67″
        Maker: Unknown; Santa Fe, New Mexico
        Date: c. 1880
    Material: Velvet edge and centers, satins
       Value: $125.00 - $200.00

Photo # 302

      Design: **The Log Patch**
        Date: c. 1890
  Condition: Fragile
    Material: Red, blue and pink prints
       Value: $150.00 - $250.00

Photo # 297 Courtesy of Helen Marshall, Doylestown, Ohio

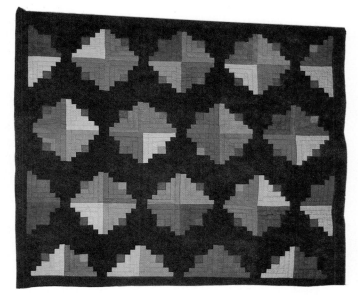

Photo # 298 Courtesy Joy Newman,
Ashland, Ohio

Photo # 299 Courtesy Kendall Scally,
Louisville, Ky.

Photo # 300

Photo # 301

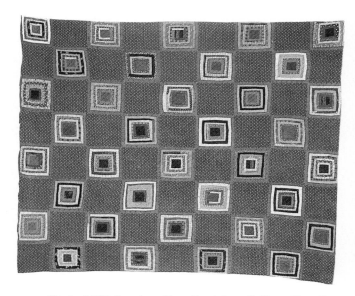

Photo # 302 Courtesy Mrs. Frank Lovell, Versailles, Ky.

Log Cabin

Photo # 303

Design: **Maltese Cross** (Pineapple, often mistaken for a Spider Web)
Size: 55″ x 65″
Date: c. 1900
Material: Wools and velvets
Value: $450.00 - $650.00

Photo # 304

Design: **Court House Steps** (fixed on a diagonal and sashed to look like Necktie - very unusual)
Size: 76″ x 88″
Maker: Unknown; Kentucky
Date: c. 1885
Value: $1,000.00

Photo # 305

Design: **Diamond Explosion** (my name - I've never seen one like it)
Type: Couch throw
Size: 46″ x 65″
Maker: Unknown; Indiana
Date: c. 1940
Material: Silks and satins
Value: $450.00 - $700.00

Photo # 306

Design: **Log Cabin Block** (like colors butted to form crosses)
Size: 58½″ x 61½″
Date: c. 1875
Material: Wool, wool challis, velvet ribbon
Value: $900.00 - $1,100.00

Comments: There is a table cover of this design touted in the Victorian needlework book *Treasures in Needlework*, 1871.

Photo # 307

Design: **Falling Timbers** (Straight Furrow)
Size: 82″ x 86″
Date: c. 1885
Material: Silks, velvets, sateen backing
Value: $2,800.00 - $3,500.00 (owner appraised)

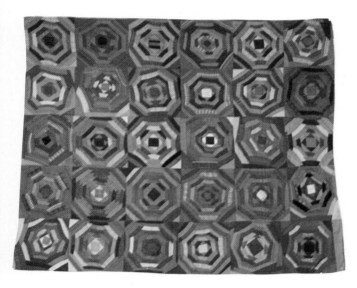

Photo # 303 Courtesy Rod Lich and Susan Parrett, "Folkways", Georgetown, Ind.

Photo # 304 Courtesy Rod Lich and Susan Parrett, "Folkways", Georgetown, Ind.

Photo # 305 Courtesy Rod Lich and Susan Parrett, "Folkways", Georgetown, Ind.

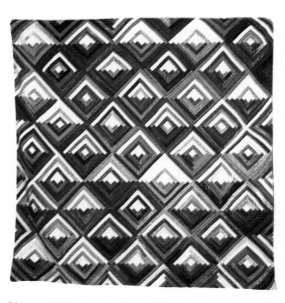

Photo # 306 Courtesy Rod Lich and Susan Parrett, "Folkways", Georgetown, Ind.

Photo # 307 Courtesy Spirit of America, St. Louis, Mo.

Necktie

Photo # 308

Design: Dad's Bow Tie
Size: 64″ x 76″
Maker: Thought to be Mennonite
Date: c. 1910
Quilting: Fleurettes and cable border
Value: $450.00 - $750.00

Photo # 309

Design: Necktie
Size: 67½″ x 77½″
Maker: Mrs. "Mote" Durbin, Estill County, Kentucky
Date: c. 1885
Condition: Machine edge, fabrics deteriorating
Quilting: Outline
Value: $75.00 - $100.00

Photo # 310

Design: Friendship Bow Tie
Size: 61″ x 89″
Maker: Estelle Bell, Berry, Kentucky
Date: 1938
Condition: Faded, block fabrics worn
Value: $50.00 - $75.00

Photo # 311

Design: Dad's Bow Tie
Size: 65″ x 78″
Maker: Unknown; Indiana
Date: c. 1890
Condition: Never washed
Material: Blue and white star fabric with pink cherry sprigged fabric
Value: $250.00 - $300.00

Photo # 312

Design: Small Bow Tie
Size: 70″ x 75″
Date: c. 1920
Material: Cotton flannel backing
Value: $150.00 - $200.00

Photo # 313

Design: Father's Silk Ties
Type: Quilt made entirely of flattened men's ties
Size: 67½″ x 76½″
Maker: Effie Lawrence, Owen County, Kentucky
Date: c. 1970
Value: $150.00 - $200.00

Comments: While made c. 1970, "some of those ties could've been nearly as old as Dad!"

Photo # 308 Courtesy Joe Saxon

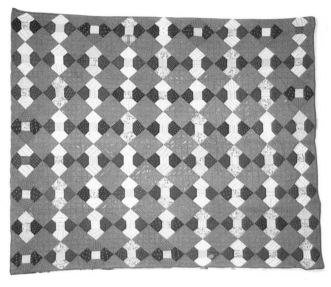

Photo # 309 Courtesy Mr. and Mrs. Maurice Rice,
Lexington, Ky.

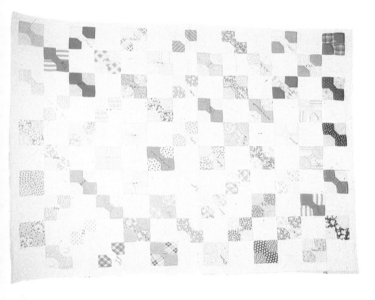

Photo # 310 Courtesy Mr. and Mrs. James Calhoun, Lexington, Ky.

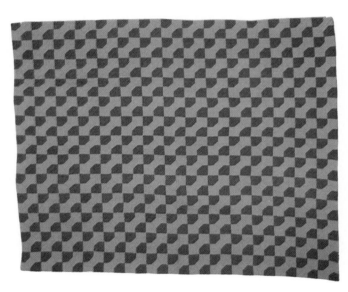

Photo # 311 Purchased from Mary Pharr, Sullivan, Ind.

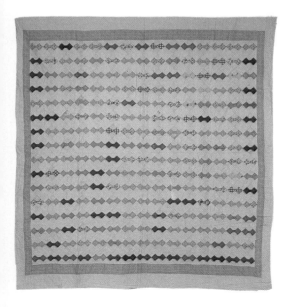

Photo # 312 Courtesy Esther Hyer,
Washington Court House, Ohio

Photo # 313 Courtesy Mr. and Mrs. Atwood Ayers, Owenton, Ky.

179

Princess Feather/Ships

Photo # 314

Design: **Princess Feather** (Star and Plume, Ben Hur's Chariot Wheel)
Maker: Unknown; Dubois County, Indiana
Value: $450.00 - $650.00

Comments: This enlarged version of the pattern is often seen in this county.

Photo # 315

Design: **Princess Feather**
Type: Possibly a 1930's kit
Size: 73½" square
Condition: Very fragile
Quilting: Shell
Value: $75.00 - $100.00

Photo # 316

Design: **The Mayflower**
Size: 90½" x 110"
Date: c. 1920
Value: $350.00 - $400.00

Comments: This was a family quilt that was tiny and unusable. They had it successfully enlarged. In fact, having seen the original, I could hardly believe it was the same quilt. Notice the sails going the wrong way and the hasty sashing. It was utilitarian. Enlargement has softened the flaws and made them charming.

Photo # 317

Design: **Chimo II**
Size: 83" x 97"
Date: Modern
Material: Polished cotton top in red, white and blue
Value: $45.00 - $70.00

Photo # 314 Courtesy Ruth Margarida, Jasper, Ind.

Photo # 315

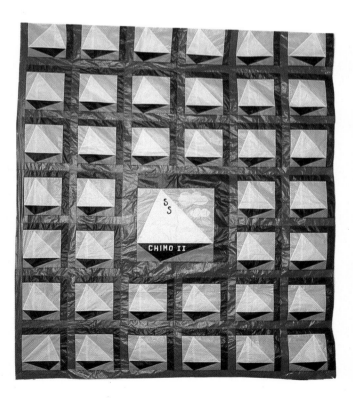

Photo # 316 Courtesy John and Trannie Davis, Acworth, Ga.

Photo # 317

Pictorial

Photo # 318

Design: **Calves** (as in Dairy Cow)
Type: Pictorial Patchwork
Size: 63" x 68"
Date: c. 1920
Condition: Good
Quilting: Outline
Value: $800.00 - $1,100.00

Comments: This is an interesting folk art quilt. I'll bet this was made for a child in the country who had a cow as a pet. It would be a way to "keep" the pet long after she'd grown up or been sold. The face is really well rendered; and there's definite design skill here, making the calf quite visible with very few fabric pieces!

Photo # 319

Design: **Horse**
Type: Pictorial Patchwork
Size: 78" square
Date: c. 1930
Condition: Good
Quilting: Outline
Value: $3,000.00 - $4,000.00 (owner appraised)

Comments: This is a great piece of textile folk art that has been fashioned with tiny square patches. Two such commercial designs were seen in newspaper quilt patterns of the 1930's; they were the Democratic Donkey and the Republican Elephant. I suspect this Tennessee(?) quilter got her idea for this horse from those.

Looking closely, she's surrounded the horse with a fence of capital T patterns, for the Tennessee Walking Horse she designed. The folks around Shelbyville, Tennessee, can tell you that a horse in that stance with that leg in that position is definitely one of theirs! She's also suggested in that "fence" that horse training takes a lot of patience, because there's one block of Patience Corners. There are also two blocks of Double Z's. I'm a little fuzzy on this, but I think this is one of the training patterns or one of the routines they perform in front of the judges.

The really "neat" thing I find in this quilt is the work suggestion. She didn't run out of black fabric; that's the dust raised by the training routine; and you can see the sweat and lather worked across the horse's chest and back from the rigorous routine he's being trained to perform.

I repeat, this is a fabulous piece of textile folk art. It's a shame we've lost its creator.

Photo # 320

Design: **Indian and Indian Symbols**
Type: Pictorial Applique
Size: 74" x 91"
Date: c. 1950
Condition: Excellent
Quilting: Straight line
Value: $800.00 - $1,100.00

Comments: This is a marvelous quilt. I suspect it's been made in the last 30 years because of the rounded edges. Quilts are integral parts of Indian manhood and burial ceremonies.

Photo # 321

Design: **Map**
Type: Applique
Size: 72" x 87"
Condition: Excellent
Quilting: Diamonds
Value: $1,500.00 - $2,000.00

Comments: Map quilts are not often encountered.

Photo # 318 Courtesy Shelly Zegart's Quilts, Louisville, Ky.

Photo # 319 Courtesy Shelly Zegart's Quilts, Louisville, Ky.

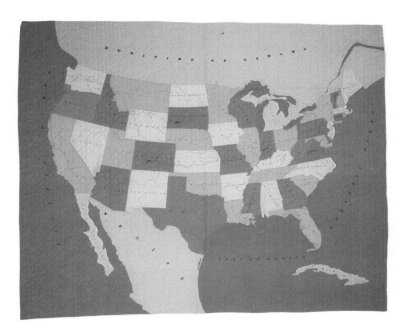

Photo # 321 Courtesy Shelly Zegart's Quilts, Louisville, Ky.

Photo # 320 Courtesy Shelly Zegart's Quilts, Louisville, Ky.

Pillows/Cigarette Inserts

Photo # 322

Design: Heart, Bear's Paw, Stencil Basket, Star Within A Star
Type: Patchwork and Stencil
Size: Various
Maker: Audrey Humphrey made the Bear's Paw
Date: 1983
Condition: Excellent
Value: $10.00 - $35.00

Comments: These are the types of pillows that are appearing more and more frequently on the market. The heart is made from an old quilt; the Bear is a quilter's "joke," the Bear with the Bear's Paw patchwork design. The stencil is a commercial print made just for pillows that can be bought in any fabric store for about $3.50 (for just the stamped top). The red Heart is a machine applique made from new fabrics placed on old pillow and feather mattress ticking, giving it the country look so popular in today's decorating schemes.

Photo # 323

Design: Cat
Value: $20.00 - $30.00

Photo # 324

Design: Cigarette Insert
Type: Pillow
Size: 16″ x 21″
Value: $25.00 - $40.00

Comments: In the years preceding World War I (c. 1912-1915), several cigarette companies included silk and flannel "blanket" inserts in their cigarette packets expressly for use in making patchwork pillow slips, tablespreads and quilts. These were blatant lures to female buyers. (Few women openly smoked cigarettes then!) The inserts included views of flags, generals, butterflies, animals, college pennants, etc. All these items are collectible today in their own right, bringing 50 cents to $2.00 each depending on the design and condition. Card collectors find these patches "worthless" if they've been sewn! Quilt collectors, on the other hand, are charmed by these easily dated quilts and pillow slips.

Photo # 325

Design: Cigarette Insert
Type: Patchwork Fragment
Value: $20.00

Comments: This is a six "blanket" flag patchwork fragment. I've heard of an entire quilt of these selling for $1,500.00 several years ago. Again, these are "types" of quilts and are collectible as such.

Photo # 322

Photo # 323 Courtesy Trannie Davis, Acworth, Ga.

Photo # 324

Photo # 325

Small Quilts

Photo # 326

Design: **Twin Dutch Boy and Girl**
Type: Tied comfort
Size: 34″ x 59″
Value: $175.00 - $250.00 pair

Photo # 327

Design: **Cottontail**
Size: 34″ x 41½
Condition: Some stains
Value: $25.00 - $50.00

Photo # 328

Design: **Colonial Basket**
Date: c. 1900
Quilting: Ribbon bound
Value: $500.00 - $750.00

Photo # 329

Design: **Springtime Blossom** (Lazy Daisy, Petal Quilt, Wheel of Fortune, Borrow and Return, Tennessee Snowball, Hearts and Gizzards)
Date: c. 1935
Material: Pink and white
Value: $75.00 - $125.00

Photo # 330

Design: **Tumbling Blocks** (Baby Blocks, Cube Work, Tea Box, Pandora's Box, Box Quilt)
Maker: Eula Weaver
Date: c. 1885
Condition: Some silks frayed
Value: $125.00 - $175.00

Photo # 331

Design: **Le Moyne Star**
Date: c. 1935
Value: $45.00 - $75.00

Photo # 326 Courtesy Rick Norton and David Cowden

Photo # 327 Courtesy Helen Marshall, Doylestown, Ohio

Photo # 328 Courtesy Mrs. Frank Lovell, Versailles, Ky.

Photo # 329 Courtesy Aubrey Humphrey, Kent, Ohio

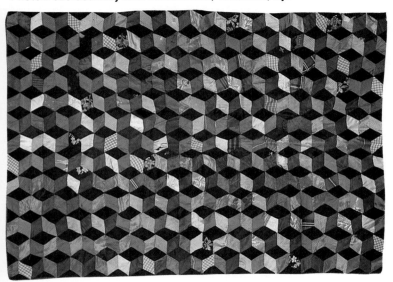

Photo # 330 Courtesy Mr. and Mrs. James Gay, Versailles, Ky.

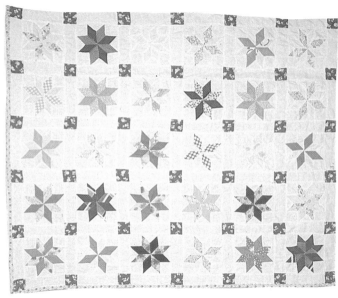

Photo # 331

Small Quilts

Photo # 332

Design: **Unknown**
Type: Applique
Size: 19″ x 23½″
Maker: ''Blanche''
Date: ''1933''
Condition: Average; faded
Quilting: Circles; almost stippled in the center
Value: $35.00 - $50.00

Comments: This appears to have been made by a child. The flowers were probably cut by her also. It may or may not have been for her doll's bed. It was the fashion then to make appliqued table scarves for lamp tables and such; but that activity was usually carried out by the lady of the house with greater skill than this piece shows.

Photo # 333

Design: **Wood Lily Variation** (Indian Head)
Size: 18″ x 19″
Material: Brown polished cotton backing
Quilting: Machine quilted
Value: $95.00 - $125.00

Comment: Basting stitches still present.

Photo # 334

Design: **Nine Patch Crib** (Irish Chain look)
Date: c. 1933
Value: $110.00 - $150.00

Design: **Burgoyne Surrounded Crib**
Date: c. 1933
Material: Pink and blue
Value: $110.00 - $150.00

Design: **Nursery Rhyme Embroidered Patches Crib**
Date: c. 1935
Value: $35.00 - $65.00

Design: **Log Cabin Doll** (Barn Raising)
Size: 23″ x 24″
Date: c. 1910
Value: $125.00 - $175.00

Design: **Crazy Patch**
Date: c. 1890
Condition: Unfinished top
Value: $35.00 - $60.00

Photo # 335

Design: **Fishing Freddie**
Size: 52½″ x 72½″
Date: 1969
Value: $125.00 - $150.00

Photo # 336

Design: **Old King Cole**
Date: c. 1945
Value: $65.00 - $100.00

Comments: Youth bed coverings are not as commonly found as are crib quilts; so far, however, the market value of these has not reflected their relative scarcity.

Photo # 332

Photo # 333 Courtesy Bill and Bunny Nolt,
Worthington, Ohio

Photo # 334 Dresser, Armand Marseilles doll, commemorative Steiff
bear and Victorian bed courtesy Mrs. Arlene Showalter, Doylestown,
Ohio; Log Cabin Doll and Crazy Patch quilts courtesy Mrs. Irene
Gilcrist, Doylestown, Ohio

Photo # 335 Courtesy Troy Chadwell Florence,
Lexington, Ky.

Photo # 336

Stamped/"Scissor"/Swastika

Photo # 337

Design: Turkey Tracks Variation
Type: Kit quilt
Size: 87″ x 89″
Date: 1982
Value: $250.00 - $300.00

Comments: Pattern pre-stamped by factory; sold in square patches which you sew together and quilt.

Photo # 338

Design: Flower Garden (French Bouquet, Honey Comb)
Type: Kit quilt
Size: 68″ x 82″
Date: c. 1940
Quilting: Shell
Value: $30.00 - $50.00

Comments: The pattern is pre-stamped by factory in yard goods. Four pieces have been sewn together here. This is the type you don't mind your children playing on at the beach.

Photo # 339

Design: Pieced Star (Star Puzzle)
Size: 64″ x 73″
Value: $15.00 - $25.00, depending on how much is still useable

Comments: This pattern is similar to the Barbara Fritchie Star (Union heroine who refused to lower her flag); it is also a variation of the Martha Washington Star. The quilt still has useful squares that can be made into pillows and stuffed animals.

Photo # 340

Design: Swastika
Condition: This quilt has about a dozen useful blocks of fabric from early 1900
Value: $15.00 - $25.00

Photo # 341

Design: Pure Symbol of Right Doctrine (Battle Ax of Thor, Catch Me If You Can, Wind Power of the Osages, Mound Builders, Favorite of the Peruvians, Chinese 10,000 Perfections, Heart's Seal)*
Size: 61½″ x 80″
Date: c. 1925
Quilting: Medallions, hearts in corners, 10 stitches to the inch
Value: $400.00 - $500.00

Comments: After Nazi Germany flew this as its flag, it was virtually abandoned as a quilter's design. The design was formerly considered to be a "good luck" symbol and is frequently seen on fabrics and postcards pre-dating World War I. This and another in blue were made by a lady of German descent.

*Hall, Carrie. *Romance of the Patchwork Quilt in America*, pg. 94, No. 21.

Photo # 342

Design: Swastika (Windmill, Devil's Dark House, Devil's Puzzle, Fly Foot, Winding Blades)
Size: 70″ x 85″
Maker: German lady; Ohio
Date: c. 1900
Condition: Fading, "obvious flaw"
Quilting: Diamonds and interlocking petal flower
Value: $75.00 - $100.00

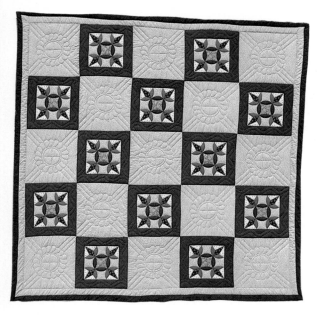

Photo # 337 Courtesy Trannie Davis, Acworth, Ga.

Photo # 338

Photo # 339

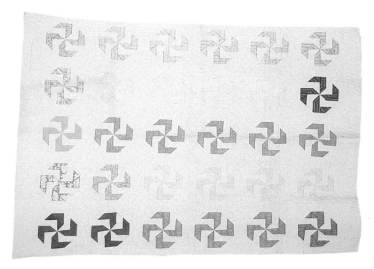

Photo # 340

Photo # 341

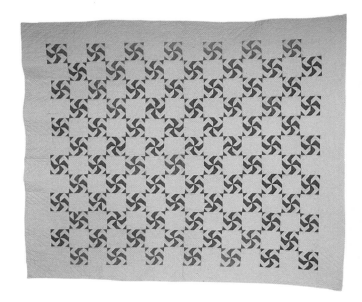

Photo # 342

191

Stars

Photo # 343

Design: **Blazing Star** (Liberty Star, Four Pointed Star)
Size: 70" x 82"
Maker: Effie Jane Wilkinson, Bloomfield, Iowa
Value: $1,800.00 - $2,000.00

Photo # 344

Design: **Star with Diamonds** (*Grandmother Clark's Patchwork Quilt Designs,* Bk. 20, 1931, W.L.M. Clark, Inc., St. Louis)
Maker: Josephine Arnold, Russellville, Kentucky
Value: $225.00 - $300.00

Comments: Other similar patterns include: Octagonal Star, Dutch Rose, Double Star, Carpenter's Wheel, Star Within A Star, Morning Star and Lone Star of Paradise. The pattern name changes with the color schemes used as well as the basic shape of the block itself. My son thinks its the best quilt we have!

Photo # 345

Design: **The Star Garden**
Maker: Unknown; Western Kentucky
Date: c. 1946
Value: $125.00 - $150.00

Photo # 346

Design: **Lone Star in Rainbow Star Motif**
Size: 76" x 90"
Date: 1930's top
Quilting: By Amish lady in straight line quilting with diamond motifs in center square
Value: $800.00 - $1,100.00

Comments: Notice the tiny star border! I have seen these tops alone priced at $295.00.

Photo # 347

Design: **Eight Pointed Star with Pointed Star Border**
Size: 72" x 79"
Date: 1860 and 1930
Quilting: ½" diamond
Value: $250.00 - $325.00

Comments: Older quilt, possibly 1860's judging from the ½" diamond quilting, which was reworked in 1930's when border was added and new stars placed over older ones . . . a successful renovation.

Photo # 348

Design: **Texas Star**
Size: 72" x 100"
Maker: Mother of Mrs. Oberhalt, Norton, Ohio
Date: c. 1936
Quilting: Emphasizes the cube formed by joining the blocks
Value: $350.00 - $500.00

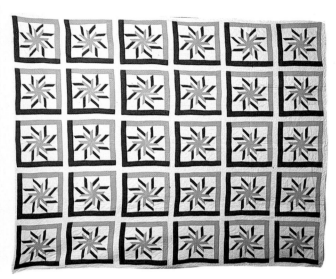

Photo # 343 Courtesy Spirit of America, St. Louis, Mo.

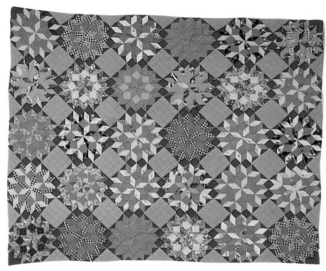

Photo # 344

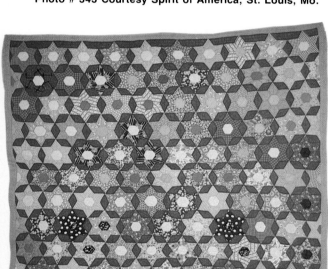

Photo # 345

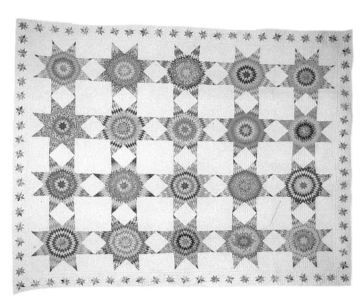

Photo # 346 Courtesy Arlene Showalter, Doylestown, Ohio

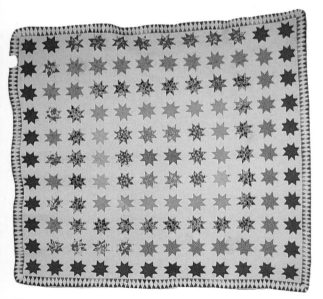

Photo # 347 Courtesy Wash's Antiques and Framing Shop,
Owenton, Ky.

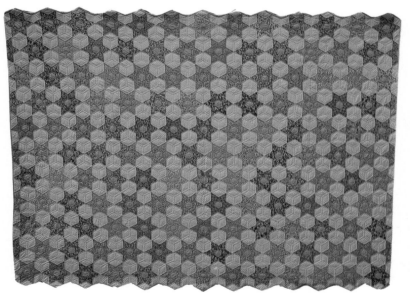

Photo # 348 Courtesy Charles and Helen Dishong, Akron, Ohio

193

Stars, Four Point

Photo # 349

Design: Guiding Star
Size: 72" x 86½"
Date: c. 1975
Value: $250.00 - $400.00

Photo # 350

Design: Triple Star Burst
Size: 70" x 87"
Maker: Unknown; Hayesville, Indiana
Date: c. 1950
Value: $350.00 - $450.00

Photo # 351

Design: Evening Stars
Date: c. 1900
Material: Shirting fabric
Value: $250.00 -$350.00

Photo # 352

Design: The Philadelphia Patch (The Pine Burr Quilt, Cockleburr)
Size: 65" x 78½"
Date: c. 1925
Condition: Average
Value: $150.00 - $250.00

Photo # 353

Design: Rocky Road to Kansas
Type: Tied comfort
Maker: Unknown; Northern Ohio
Date: c. 1910
Condition: Good, very thick
Value: $225.00 - $325.00

Photo # 354

Design: Unknown; possibly Philadelphia Patch Variation
Size: 64½" x 77½"
Maker: Unknown; Northern Ohio
Date: c. 1890
Value: $175.00 - $250.00

Photo # 349 Courtesy Shirley Graff, Brunswick, Ohio

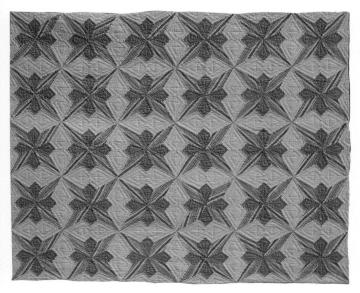

Photo # 350 Courtesy Ruth Margarida, Jasper, Ind.

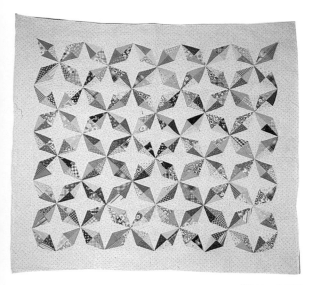

Photo # 351

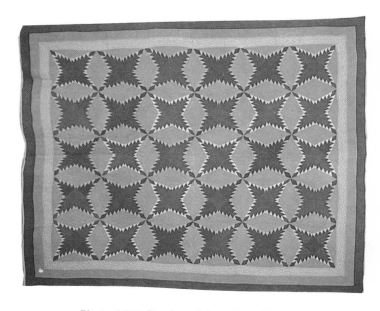

Photo # 352 Purchased from Mary Pharr, Sullivan, Ind.

Photo # 353

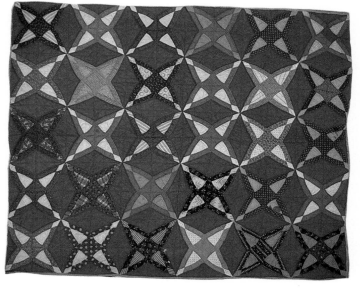

Photo # 354

Trees

Photo # 355

Design: Tree of Paradise
Size: 66″ x 79″
Date: c. 1880
Quilting: Medallion, winding leaf border, 12 stitches to the inch
Value: $400.00 - $650.00

Photo # 356

Design: Tree of Paradise
Size: 70½″ x 85½″
Date: c. 1900
Quilting: Medallion, 8 stitches per inch
Value: $400.00 - $600.00

Photo # 357

Design: Tree of Paradise (Sawtooth edging)
Size: 69″ x 82¼″
Maker: Unknown; Gainesville, Florida
Date: c. 1880
Condition: Obvious flaw, some bleeding of blue fabrics
Quilting: Winding leaf border
Value: $325.00 - $550.00

Photo # 355 Courtesy Katy Harpster, Ashland, Ohio

Photo # 356

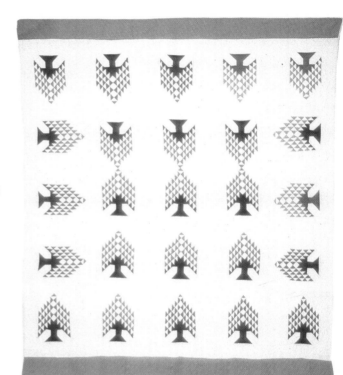

Photo # 357 Purchased from Marlene Oberst, The Shop, Micanopy, Fla.

Wall Hangings

Photo # 358

Design: Roman Stripe
Type: Patchwork
Size: 47″ x 56″
Maker: Caron Mosey
Date: 1983
Condition: Excellent
Quilting: Florals, tulip corners, corded center star
Value: $210.00 - $300.00

Comments: Caron was working to get an Amish look to her Roman Stripe wall hanging. At the same time, she wanted to challenge the stripes with a ''design'' which she brought into the piece with the star and the floral quilting.

Photo # 359

Design: The Feather Edged Star
Type: Patchwork
Size: 35″ square
Date: c. 1983
Condition: Excellent
Quilting: Outline
Value: $45.00 - $85.00

Comments: This was a gift from a friend who bought it at a crafts show, so I can't credit the maker. Wall hangings are very popular right now; and this one is made in excellent ''earth tones'' and has a greatly admired pattern.

Photo # 358 Courtesy Caron Mosey, Flushing, Mich.

Photo # 359

Late Arrivals

Photo # 360

Design: Flower Album Chintz
Type: Applique
Origin: New England
Date: c. 1840
Condition: Excellent
Value: $2,300.00 - $2,700.00

Comments: It was the style of this era to cut floral designs from chintz fabric and applique them onto a quilt top. It's referred to as Broderie Perse (after the Persian manner) and usually it involves an elaborate, bed-covering, Tree of Life design which was a much-admired type of Persian or Indian spread known as a palampore. You seldom see the technique used today although I did run into one quilt from the 1930's that had chintz blue ribboned bows applied in this fashion. I suspect it had been done to match some bedroom wall paper.

Photo # 361

Design: Log House With Rail Fence
Type: Patchwork and Applique
Origin: Lancaster, Ohio
Date: c. 1930
Value: $350.00 - $450.00

Comments: You can recognize that this is not one of your run-of-the-mill quilt tops. This has dynamic graphics!

Photo # 362

Design: Eagles With Sears Building
Type: Applique
Origin: Toledo, Ohio
Date: 1933
Condition: Excellent
Quilting: Airplanes, refrigerators, trolley car (things reflecting a "Century of Progress")
Value: $3,500.00 - $5,000.00

Comments: This quilt was made in response to the Sears' Company contest theme, "Century of Progress" in connection with the 1933 World's Fair held in Chicago, Illinois. It's the type of quilt that has extraordinary investment potential. It's one of a kind; it has unique quilting patterns; it has EAGLES, ever desirable in quilt collecting circles; it has a SEAR'S BUILDING featured at the center (you got extra money for that if your quilt won) which guarantees interest in the quilt. (How many thousands of people are employed by that company?) It has history and superb "connections;" and beyond all that, it's a great looking quilt!

Were I an investor purchasing this quilt, I'd expect marketable value to rise dramatically; collecting quilted "art" is still in its infancy and present marketable values may not reflect the true value of exceptional historic pieces.

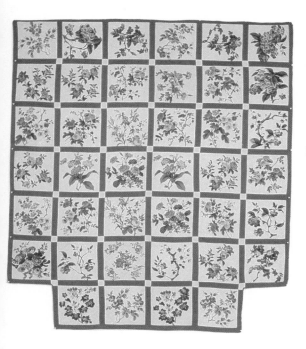

Photo # 360

Photo # 361

Photo # 362 Photo courtesy Sandra Mitchell, American Horse
Antiques and Folk Art, Chambley, Mich.

Late Arrivals

Photo # 363

Design: Delectable Mountains With Applique Border
Type: Patchwork and Applique
Size: 70″ x 89″
Origin: Pennsylvania
Date: c. 1865
Value: $700.00 - $950.00

Comments: The maker of this took a graphic pattern and made it superb by adding the border appliques. Today's quilters need to pay more attention to their border treatments. Proper borders can make a good quilt great!

One national quilting judge I spoke with told me that more quilts are marked down on border techniques than any other single thing. She added, too, that while it was once a virtue and a necessity to make quilts from scrap fabrics, today's quilter should not feel bound to that tradition. Many quilts, she said, are down-graded because inferior fabrics are employed in their makeup. If your quilt is to hang on some future collector's wall as an example of today's quilting art, use the best materials you can afford, in the best design and color arrangement you can achieve; and please sign and date your work. Happy Quilting . . . and collecting!

Photo # 364

Design: Le Moyne Star (Center Medallion)
Type: Patchwork and Applique
Size: 84″ square
Maker: Rachael Vanderheyden, New York
Date: 1848
Value: $2,800.00 - $3,300.00

Photo # 363 Photo courtesy Sandra Mitchell
and Merry Silber

Photo # 364 Photo courtesy of Sandra Mitchell, American Horse
Antiques & Folk Art, Chambley, Michigan

BIBLIOGRAPHY

"A Celebration of Quilting." *The Buckeye Marketeer,* Sept., 1983, pp. 6-7.

"Aberfoyle Fabrics." *McCall's Magazine,* (April, 1928), p. 133.

----------. *McCall's Magazine,* (June, 1928), p. 99.

"Another Kentucky Heritage - Quilts." *Back Home in Kentucky* (July/Aug., 1981), p. 16

Albacete, M.J. et al. *Ohio Quilts: A Living Tradition.* Canton, Ohio: The Canton Art Institute, 1981.

Appel, David H. (ed.). *An Album for Americans.* New York: Crown Publishers, Inc., 1983.

Bacon, Lenice Ingram. *American Patchwork Quilts.* New York: Wm. Morrow & Co., Inc., 1973.

Baker, M. T. "Quilts of Quality Worth Their Weight in Diamonds, Circles and Squares." *Tri-State Trader,* April 2, 1984, pp. 1, 48

Bank, Mirra. *Anonymous Was A Woman.* New York: St. Martin's Press, 1979.

Benson, Nancy C. "The Art of Quilting is Reviving." *The Buckeye Marketeer,* Sept., 1983, pp. 1; 7.

Berman, Eleanor. "Quilts: Warm? They're Positively Hot." *The Robb Report,* (April, 1984), pp. 48-59.

Better Homes and Gardens Patchwork Quilting. Des Moines, Iowa: Meredith Corporation, 1977.

Beyer Jinny. *The Quilter's Album of Blocks and Borders.* McLean, Va.: EPM Publications, Inc., 1980.

Birney, Dion. "The Marketplace: Quilts." *Arts and Antiques,* (Sept./Oct., 1983), pp. 26, 28, 29.

Bishop, Robert. *New Discoveries in American Quilts.* New York: E.P. Dutton & Co., 1975.

----------. *Quilts.* New York: Alfred A. Knopf, 1982.

Blondel, Elisabeth May. "The New Raised Quilting's the Thing." *McCall's Magazine.* (Sept., 1928), p. 136.

----------. "Quilting in Blocks a New Vogue." *McCall's Magazine,* (Feb., 1928), p. 127

Bonesteel, Georgia. *Lap Quilting.* Birmingham: Oxmoor House, Inc., 1982.

Brightbill, Dorothy. *Quilting as a Hobby.* N.Y.: Bonanza Books, 1963.

Buffalo Bill Historical Center, Cody, Wyoming. New York: Visual West, 1977.

Burdick, J.R. (ed.). *The American Card Catalogue.* New York: Nostalgia Press, 1967. pp. 83-88.

Bush, Ann McReynolds. "Quilters of the Hudson Valley." *1001 Decorating Ideas,* (July/Aug., 1976), pp. 50-55.

Christopherson, Katy. "Glimpses of Kentucky History." *Back Home in Kentucky,* (Jan./Feb., 1983), pp. 4-5.

----------. "Kentucky's Own Carrie Hall, Linda Lowe." *Back Home in Kentucky,* (Nov./Dec., 1982), pp. 8-9.

----------. "Sunburst in A Garden Maze." *Back Home in Kentucky,* (July/Aug., 1981), pp. 16-17.

----------. "A Star Blazes in Shepardsville." *Back Home in Kentucky,* (Nov./Dec., 1981), pp. 28-29.

----------. "Capturing Time and Place in a Quilt." *Back Home in Kentucky,* (May/June, 1982), pp. 8-9.

Clabburn, Pamela. *Patchwork.* Aylesbury, Bucks HP17 9AJ, UK: Shire Publications Ltd., 1983.

Clarke, Mary Washington. *Kentucky Quilts and Their Makers.* Lexington, Ky.: The University Press of Kentucky, 1976.

Colby, Averil. *Patchwork Quilts.* London: B.T.Batsford, Ltd., 1965.

Colgan, Susan. "Collecting Quilts: Where It All Began." *Arts and Antiques,* (Sept./Oct., 1983), pp. 51-53.

Conley, Mary Ann. "Step Back in Time." *Collector's Marketplace,* (Oct., 1983), pp. 12-15.

Cooper, Patricia and Norma Bradley Buferd. *The Quilters.* Garden City, N.Y.: Anchor Press/Doubleday, 1978.

Decorating & Craft Ideas. Fort Worth: Decorating and Craft Ideas (Feb., 1976).

Echols, Margit. "The Patchwork Puzzle." *Games,* (Dec. 1983), pp. 26-27.

Emmerling, Mary Ellisor. *Collecting American Country.* New York: Clarkson N. Pottery, Inc., 1983.

Finley, Ruth. *Old Patchwork Quilts and the Women Who Made Them.* Newton Center, Mass.: Charles T. Branford Co., 1971.

Fry, Annette Riley. "Bedspread in the Mountain Manner." *Americana,* (May/June, 1978), pp. 28-32.

Gilberg, Laura S. & Barbara B. Buchholz. *Needlepoint Design from Amish Quilts.* New York: Charles Scribner's Sons, 1977.

Ginnings, Daphne. "Quilts Can Be Rich in History." *Beacon Journal,* Oct. 2, 1983, pp. 4-6.

Goodman, L.M. *Old Quilts: Patchwork Designs.* Watkins Glen, N.Y.: The American Life Foundation and Study Institute, 1972.

Grandmother Clark's Patchwork Quilt Designs from Books 20-23. St. Louis: W. L. M. Clark, Inc., 1934.

Haders, Phyllis. *Quilts.* Pittstown, N.J.: The Main Street Press, 1981.

Hall, Carrie and Rose G. Kretsinger. *The Romance of the Patchwork Quilt in America.* New York: Bonanza Books, 1935.

Hall, Eliza Calvert. *A Book of Hand-Woven Coverlets.* Boston: Little, Brown & Co., 1914.

Harding, Deborah and Robert L. Anderson. "Pennsylvania Dutch." *Family Circle,* (Oct., 1974), pp. 123-134; 194; 196; 198; 200-01; 203-04; 210-12.

Hassel, Carla J. *You Can Be a Super Quilter.* Des Moines, Iowa: Wallace Homestead, 1980.

----------. *Super Quilter II.* Des Moines, Iowa: Wallace Homestead, 1982.

Heirloom Quilts and Spreads for Applique, for Patchwork. Grand Rapids, Mich.: Needleart Guild (n.d.).

Henninger, Daniel, and Manuela Hoelterhoff. "The Art of People on the Run."

Hinson, Dolores. *Quilting Manual.* New York: Dover Publications, Inc. 1966.

Holstein, Jonathan. *The Pieced Quilt An American Design Tradition.* New York: Galahad Books, 1973.

Holstein, Jonathan, and John Finley. *Kentucky Quilts, 1800-1900.* Louisville, Ky.: The Kentucky Quilt Project, Inc., 1982.

Ickis, Marguerite. *The Standard Book of Quilt Making and Collecting.* New York: Dover Publications, Inc., 1949.

Jackson-Meyer, Suellen. "Lone Star." *Star of Texas Sentinel,* Sept., 1982, pg. 6.

James, Michael. "Color in Quilts." *Quilter's Newsletter Magazine,* (Apr., 1977), pp. 16-17.

Johnson, Mary Elizabeth. *Country Quilt Patterns.* Birmingham, Ala.: Oxmoor House, 1977.

----------. *Prize Country Quilts.* Birmingham, Ala.: Oxmoor House, 1979.

Jones, Betty. "Quilt Blocks." *The Progressive Farmer* (Mar., 1961), pg. 82.

Kentucky Quilt Calendar, 1983. Lexington, Ky. Kentucky Heritage Quilt Society.

Khin, Yvonne M. *Quilt Names and Patterns.* Washington, D.C.: Acropolis Books, Ltd., 1980.

Kiracofe, Roderick and Michael. *The Quilt Digest.* San Francisco: Kiracofe and Kile, 1983.

Lady's Circle Patchwork Quilts. Nos. 1-3; 23; 31. New York: Ladies Circle Inc. 1973; 1974; 1975; 1981; 1983.

Lamphier, Mary Jane. *Patchwork Plus.* Des Moines, Iowa: Wallace Homestead Book Co., 1983.

Lane, Rose Wilder. "The Story of American Needlework #2: Patchwork." *Woman's Day* (Apr., 1961), pp. 36-41.

Laury, Jean Ray. *Quilted Clothing*. Birmingham: Oxmoor House, Inc., 1982.

----------. *Quilts & Coverlets, A Contemporary Approach*. New York:

Little, Francis. *Early American Textiles*. New York: The Century Co., 1931.

Malone, Maggie. *1001 Patchwork Designs*. New York: Sterling Publishing Co., Inc., 1942.

McAdams, Betty. *The Kansas City Star*. Little Rock, Ark.: Betty McAdams, 1982.

McCall's How to Quilt It! New York: The McCall Pattern Co., 1953.

McCall's Antique Quilts. New York: The McCall Pattern Co., 1974.

McCall's Bicentennial Quilt Book. New York: The McCall Pattern Co., 1975.

McCall's Quilt It! Book II. New York: The McCall Pattern Co., 1972.

McKim, Ruby Short. "Expressing Yourself in Your Home." *Better Homes and Gardens*, (Feb., 1929), p. 82.

----------. *One Hundred and One Patchwork Patterns*. New York: Dover Publications, Inc., 1962.

McMorris, Penny. "Crazy Quilt: A Fabric Scrapbook." *Arts and Antiques*, (Sept. /Oct., 1983), pp. 42-49.

"Mennonite Relief Sale Tops $165.000." *Farm and Dairy*, pp. 2; 10.

Montgomery, Florence M. *Printed Textiles: English and American Cottons & Linens, 1700-1850* (A Winthur Book). New York: The Viking Press, 1970.

Musheno, Elizabeth J. *Book of Colonial Needlework*. Scarborough, Ontario, Canada: Van Nostrand Reinhold Co. (Copyright 75-12166 by Litton Educational Pub., Inc., 1975.)

Needleart Guild's Original Master Quilting Patterns. Grand Rapids, Mich.: Needleart Guild, (n.d.)

"Nine Lovely Things for That Most Important Room." *McCall's Magazine*, (Mar., 1930), p. 170.

Orlofsky, Patsy and Myron, *Quilts in America*. New York: McGraw-Hill Book Company, 1974.

"Pa Ndau, The Textile Art of Hmong." Finish Yourself Pa Ndau Kits. Des Moines, Iowa: Hmong-Lao Community (P. O. Box 8298).

Patchwork Designs. Watkins Glen, N.Y.: The American Life Foundation, 1972.

Patchwork Patter, Vol. II, 1-4. Greenbelt, Md.: The National Quilting Assoc., Inc. 1983.

Patterns P-570, Vol. II. Danvers, Mass.: Tower Press, Inc., 1970.

Pellman, Rachel T. and Joanne Ranck. *Quilts Among the Plain People*. Lancaster, Pa.: Good Books, 1981.

Percival, Maciver. *The Chintz Book*. London: Wm. Heinemann, Ltd., 1923.

Peto, Florence. *American Quilts & Coverlets*. New York: Chanticleer Press, 1949.

----------. *Historic Quilts*. New York: the American Historical Co., Inc.

1965.

----------. "Old Quilts Tell A Story." *The American Home*, (July, 1983) pp. 8-10.

Pettit, Florence Harvey. *America's Printed & Painted Fabrics, 1600-1900*. New York: Hastings House, 1970.

----------. *Block Printing on Fabrics*. New York: Hastings House, 1952.

Quadriga Cloth Prints, 9-1165. Ely Fabrics, Spring 1984.

Quilt World. Seabrook, N.H.: The House of White Birches, Inc., (Oct., 1981).

Quilt. New York: Harris Publications, (Sum., 1983), Vol. 5; No. 2.

Quilter's Newsletter Magazine: (Oct. 1974, Issue #60 - Sept. 1983, Issue 155).

Quilting and Patchwork (A Sunset Book). Menlo Park, Ca.: Lane Publishing Co., 1980.

Quilts and Other Comforts, Cat. #6. Wheatridge, Co.: Leman Publications, Inc. 1975.

Reader's Digest Complete Guide to Needlework. Pleasantville, N.Y.: The Reader's Digest Association, Inc. 1979.

Riddle, Charlotte and Bruce. "Care of Older and Antique Quilts."

Roesler, Jean. *Rectangular Quilt Blocks*. Des Moines, Iowa: Wallace Homestead Book Co., 1982.

Russell, Candice. "Quilts: An American Folk Art." *Sky*, (Mar. 1984), pp. 53-60.

Safford, Carleton L. and Robert Bishop. *American's Quilts and Coverlets*. New York: Weathervane Books, 1972.

Swan, Susan Burrows. *A Winterthur Guide to American Needlework*. New York, Crown Publisher, Inc., 1976.

The Mountain Mist Blue Book of Quilts for 1938. Cincinnati, O.: The Sterns and Foster Co., 1937.

"The New McCall 'Smocktop' Pattern--A Gay Patch Quilt and the Latest Medallions." *McCall's Magazine* (Mar., 1928), pp. 130-31.

The Patchwork Book. Chicago: Manning Publishing Company, 1931.

Vote, Marjean. *Patchwork Pleasure*. Des Moines, Iowa: Wallace Homestead Book Co., (n.d.).

Vreeland, Susan. "Future of Laotian Folk Art Hangs by a Thread." San Diego: The Christian Science Monitor (Nov. 29, 1981), p. 15.

Walker, Michele. *The Pattern Library Quilting and Patchwork*. New York: Ballantine Books, 1983.

Warren and Pullman. *Treasures in Needlework*. (First Published in 1870.) New York: Berkley Publishing Corp., 1976.

Wilson, Erica. *Quilts of America*. Birmingham: Oxmoor House, Inc., 1979.

Woodard, Thos. K. & Blanche Greenstein. *Crib Quilts and Other Small Wonders*. New York: E. P. Dutton, 1981.

Wooster, Ann-Sargent. *Quiltmaking: The Modern Approach to a Traditional Craft*. New York: Galahad Books, 1972.

INDEX OF QUILTS

207

Two Important Tools For The
Astute Antique Dealer, Collector and Investor

Schroeder's Antiques Price Guide

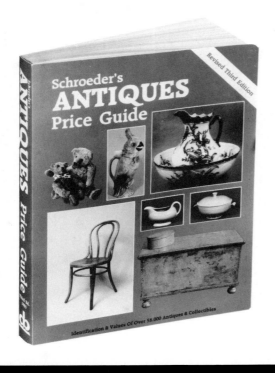

The very best low cost investment that you can make if you are really serious about antiques and collectibles is a good identification and price guide. We publish and highly recommend **Schroeder's Antiques Price Guide.** Our editors and writers are very careful to seek out and report accurate values each year. We do not simply change the values of the items each year but start anew to bring you an entirely new edition. If there are repeats, they are by chance and not by choice. Each huge edition (it weighs 3 pounds!) has over 56,000 descriptions and current values on 608 - 8½x11 pages. There are hundreds and hundreds of categories and even more illustrations. Each topic is introduced by an interesting discussion that is an education in itself. Again, no dealer, collector or investor can afford not to own this book. It is available from your favorite bookseller or antiques dealer at the low price of $9.95. If you are unable to find this price guide in your area, it's available from Collector Books, P. O. Box 3009, Paducah, KY 42001 at $9.95 plus $1.00 for postage and handling.

Schroeder's INSIDER and Price Update

A monthly newsletter published for the antiques and collectibles marketplace.

The **"INSIDER"**, as our subscribers have fondly dubbed it, is a monthly newsletter published for the antiques and collectibles marketplace. It gives the readers timely information as to trends, price changes, new finds, and market moves both upward and downward. Our writers are made up of a panel of well-known experts in the fields of Glass, Pottery, Dolls, Furniture, Jewelry, Country, Primitives, Oriental and a host of other fields in our huge industry. Our subscribers have that "inside edge" that makes them more profitable. Each month we explore 8-10 subjects that are "in", and close each discussion with a random sampling of current values that are recorded at press time. Thousands of subscribers eagerly await each monthly issue of this timely 16-page newsletter. A sample copy is available for $3.00 postpaid. Subscriptions are $24.00 for 12 months; 24 months for $45.00; 36 months for $65.00, all postpaid. A sturdy 3-ring binder to store your **Insider** is available for $5.00 postpaid. This newsletter contains NO paid advertising and is not available on your newsstand. It may be ordered by sending your check or money order to Collector Books, P. O. Box 3009, Paducah, KY 42001.